DOORYARD STORIES

Look for these other great books by Clara Dillingham
Pierson also from Living Book Press

- AMONG THE FARMYARD PEOPLE
- AMONG THE POND PEOPLE
- AMONG THE FOREST PEOPLE
- AMONG THE MEADOW PEOPLE
- AMONG THE NIGHT PEOPLE
- DOORYARD STORIES
- TALES FROM A POULTRY FARM

WWW.LIVINGBOOKPRESS.COM

This edition published 2021
by Living Book Press
Copyright © Living Book Press, 2021

ISBN: 978-1-922634-25-2 (hardcover)
        978-1-922634-26-9 (softcover)

First published in 1903.

NATIONAL
LIBRARY
OF AUSTRALIA

A catalogue record for this
book is available from the
National Library of Australia

DOORYARD STORIES

BY

CLARA DILLINGHAM PIERSON

LIVING BOOK
PRESS

CONTENTS

PREFACE

My Dear Little Friends:—These stories are of things which I have seen with my own eyes in my own yard, and the people of whom I write are my friends and near neighbors. Some of them, indeed, live under my roof, and Silvertip has long been a member of our family. So, you see, I have not had to do like some writers—sit down and think and think how to make the people act in their stories. These tales are of things which have really happened, and all I have done is to write them down for you.

Many of them have been told over and over again to my own little boy, and because he never tires of hearing of the time when Silvertip was a Kitten, and about the Wasps who built inside my shutters, I think you may care to hear also. He wants me to be sure to tell how the baby Swift tumbled down the chimney into his bedroom, and wishes you might have seen it in the little nest we made. When I tell these tales to him, I have great trouble in ending them, for there is never a time when he does not ask: "And what did he do then Mother?" But I am telling you as much as I can of how everything happened, and if there was more which I did not see and cannot describe, you will have to make up the rest to suit yourselves.

Besides, you know, there is always much which one cannot see or hear, but which one knows is happening somewhere in this beautiful great world. The birds do not stop living and working and loving when they leave us for the sunny south, and above us, around us, and even under our feet many things are done which we cannot see. As we become better acquainted with the little people who live in our dooryards, we shall see more and more interesting things, and I wish you might all grow to be like my little boy, who is never lonely or in need of a playmate so long as a Caterpillar or a Grasshopper is in sight.

See how many tiny neighbors you have around you, and how much you can learn about them. Then you will find your own dooryard as interesting as mine and know that there are playmates everywhere.

Your friend,

Clara D. Pierson.

STANTON, MICHIGAN, *October 30, 1902.*

SILVERTIP

A VERY small, wet, and hungry Kitten pattered up and down a board walk one cold and rainy night. His fur was so soaked that it dripped water when he moved, and his poor little pink-cushioned paws splashed more water up from the puddly boards every time he stepped. His tail looked like a wet wisp of fur, and his little round face was very sad. "Meouw!" said he. "Meouw! Meouw!"

He heard somebody coming up the street. "I will follow that Gentleman," he thought, "and I will cry so that he will be sorry for me and give me a home."

When this person came nearer he saw that it was not a Gentleman at all, but a Lady who could hardly keep from being blown away. He could not have seen her except that Cat's eyes can see in the dark. "Meouw!" said the Kitten. "Meouw! Meouw!"

"Poor little Pussy!" said a voice above him. "Poor little Pussy! But you must not come with me."

"Meouw!" answered he, and trotted right along after her. He was a Kitten who was not easily discouraged. He rubbed up against her foot and made her stop for fear of stepping on him. Then he felt himself gently lifted up and put aside.

He scrambled back and rubbed against her other foot. And so it was for more than two blocks. The Lady, as he always called her afterward, kept pushing him gently to one side and he kept scrambling back. Sometimes she even had to stand quite still for fear of stepping on him.

"Meouw!" said the Kitten, and he made up his mind that anybody who spoke so kindly to strange Kittens would be a good mistress. "I will stick to her," he said to himself. "I don't care how many times she pushes me away, I *will* scramble back."

When they turned in at a gate he saw a big house ahead of him with many windows brightly lighted and another light on the porch. "I like that home," he said to himself. "I will slip through the door when she opens it."

But after she had turned the key in the door she pushed him back and closed the screen between them. Then he heard her say: "Poor little Pussy! I want to take you in, but we have agreed not to adopt another Cat." Then she closed the door.

He wanted to explain that he was not really a Cat, only a little Kitten, but he had no chance to say anything, so he waited outside and thought and cried. He did not know that the Lady and her husband feared that Cats would eat the many birds who nested in the trees on the lawn. He thought it very hard luck for a tiny Kitten to be left out in the cold rain while the Lady was reading by a blazing grate fire. He did not know that as she sat by the fire she thought about him instead of her book, for she loved little Kittens, and found it hard to leave any out in the street alone.

While he was thinking and crying, a tall Gentleman with a black beard and twinkling brown eyes came striding up to the brightly lighted porch. "Well, Pussy-cat!" said the Gentleman, and took a bunch of shining, jingling things out of his pocket and stuck one of them into a little hole in the door and turned it. Then the door swung open, and the Gentleman, who was trying to close his umbrella and shake off the rain, called first to the Lady and then to the kitten. "O Clara!" he cried. "Come to see this poor little Kitten. Here Kitty, Kitty, Kitty! I know you want to see him. Here Kitty, Kitty, Kitty! I should have thought you would have heard him crying. Here Kitty, Kitty, Kitty!"

The Lady came running out and was laughing. "Yes, John," she said, "I have had the pleasure of meeting him before. He was under my feet most of the way home from church to-night, and I could hardly bear to leave him outside. But you know what we promised each other, that we would not adopt another Cat, on account of the birds."

The Gentleman sat down upon the stairs and wiped the Kitten off with his handkerchief. "Y-yes, I know," he said weakly, "but Clara, look at this poor little fellow. He couldn't catch a Chipping Sparrow."

"Not now," answered the Lady, "yet he will grow, if he is like most Kittens, and you know what we said. If we don't stick to it we will soon have as many Cats as we did a few years ago."

The Kitten saw that if he wanted to stay in this home he must insist upon it and be very firm indeed with these people. So he kept on crying and stuck his sharp claws into the Gentleman's sleeve. The Gentleman said "Ouch!" and lifted him on to his coat lapel. There he clung and shook and cried.

"Well, I suppose we mustn't keep him then," said he; "but we will give him a warm supper anyway." So they got some milk and heated it, and set it in a shallow dish before the grate. How that Kitten did eat! The Lady sat on the floor beside him, and the Gentleman drew his chair up close, and they said that it seemed hard to turn him out, but that they would have to do it because they had promised each other.

The Kitten lapped up his milk with a soft click-clicking of his little pink tongue, and then turned his head this way and that until he had licked all the corners clean. He was so full of warm milk that his sides bulged out, and his fur had begun to dry and stuck up in pointed wisps all over him. He pretended to lap milk long after it was gone. This was partly to show them how well he could wash dishes, and partly to put off the time when he should be thrust out of doors.

When he really could not make believe any longer, his tongue being so tired, he began to cry and rub against these two people. The Gentleman was the first to speak. "I cannot stand this," he said. "If he has to go, I want to get it over." He picked up the Kitten and took him to the door. As fast as he loosened one of the Kitten's claws from his coat he stuck another one in, and at last the Lady had to help get him free. "He is a regular Rough Rider," said the Gentleman. "There is no shaking him off."

The Kitten didn't understand what a Rough Rider was, but it did not sound like finding a home, so he cried some more. Then the door was shut behind him and he was alone in the porch. "Well," he said, "I like that house and those

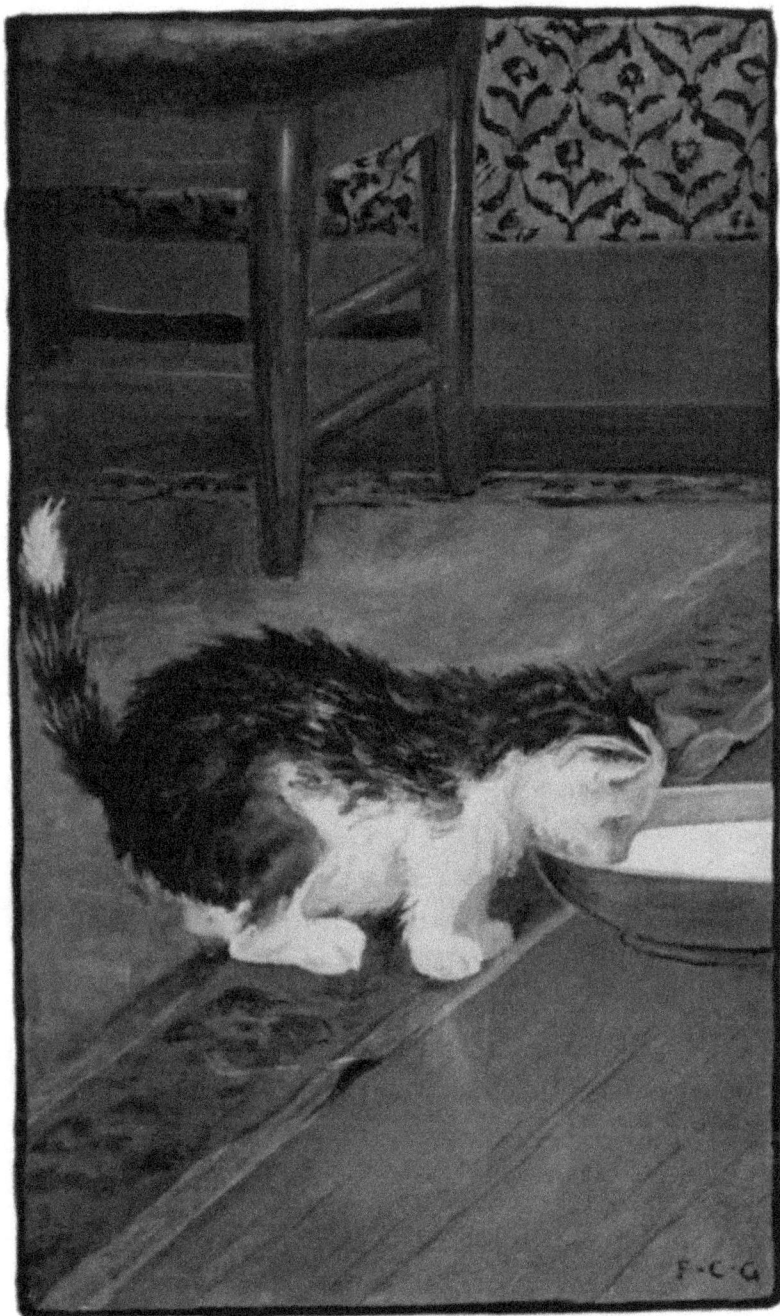

THE KITTEN LAPPED UP HIS MILK.

people, even if they did put me out. I think I will make them adopt me." So he cuddled down in a sheltered, dry corner, put his four feet all close together, and curled his tail, as far as it would go, around them. And there he stayed all night.

In the morning, when the rain had stopped and the sun was shining brightly, he trotted around the house and cried. He went up on to another porch, rubbed against the door and cried. The Maid opened the door and put out some milk for him. He could see into the warm kitchen and smell the breakfast cooking on the range. When she came out to get the empty dish, he slipped in through the open door. She said "Whish!" and "Scat!" and "Shoo!" and tried to drive him out, but he pretended not to understand and cuddled quietly down in a corner where she could not easily reach him. Just then some food began to burn on the range and the Maid let him alone. The Kitten did not cry now. He had other work to do, and began licking himself all over and scratching his ears with his hind feet.

When he heard the Gentleman and the Lady talking in the dining-room, he watched his chance and slipped in. He decided to pay the most attention to the Gentleman, for he had been the first to take him up. They were laughing and talking and saying how glad they were that the rain had stopped falling. "I believe, John," the Lady said, "that if it had not been for me, you would really have kept that Kitten last night."

"Oh, no," answered the Gentleman. "We ought not to keep Cats. I think that if it had not been for me *you* would have kept him."

Just at that minute the Kitten began climbing up his trousers leg and crying. "Poor little Pussy," said the Gentleman. "Clara, can't we spare some of this cream?" He reached for the pitcher. The Kitten began to feel more sure of a home.

"O John, not here?" began the Lady, and the Maid came in to explain how it all happened. The Kitten stuck his claws into the Gentleman's coat and would not let go. Then he cried some more and waved his tail. He had a very beautiful tail, marked just like that of a Raccoon, and he turned it toward the Lady. He had heard somewhere about putting the best foot forward, and thought that a tail might do just as well. While he was waving his tail at the Lady he rubbed his head against the Gentleman's black beard.

"If we *should* keep him, John," said the Lady, "we ought to call him Silvertip, because he has such a pretty white tip to his tail." The Kitten waved it again and began to purr.

"If you knew what a strong and fearless fellow he is, you would call him Teddy," answered the Gentleman, turning over a paper which said in big black letters, "Our Teddy Wins."

"Call him Teddy Silvertip then," said the Lady, as she reached for the bell. When the Maid came in answer to her ring, she said, "Belle, please take our Kitten into the kitchen and feed him." Then the Kitten let go and was carried away happy, for he had found a home. He had also learned how to manage the Lady and the Gentleman, and he was always *very* firm with them after that.

THE FIGHT FOR THE
BIRD-HOUSE

UNDER the cornice of the tool-house was an old cigar-box with a tiny doorway cut in one end and a small board nailed in front of it for a porch. This had been put up for a bird-house, and year after year a pair of Wrens had nested there, until they began to think it really their own. When they left it in the fall to fly south, they always looked back lovingly at it, and talked over their plans for the next summer.

"I think we might better leave this nest inside all winter," Mrs. Wren always said. "It will seem so much more home-like when we return, and it will not be much trouble to clear it out afterward."

"An excellent plan, my dear," her cheerful little husband would reply. "You remember we did so last season. Besides," he always added, "that will show other birds that Wrens have lived here, and they will know that we are expecting to return, since that is the custom in our family."

"And then do you think they will leave it for us?" Mrs. Wren would ask. "You know they might want it for themselves."

"What if they did want it?" Mr. Wren had said. "They

could go somewhere else, couldn't they? Do you suppose I would ever steal another bird's nesting-place if I knew it?"

"N-no," said Mrs. Wren, "but not everybody is as unselfish as you." And she looked at him tenderly.

The Wrens were a most devoted couple,—all in all, about the nicest birds on the place. And that was saying a great deal, for there were many nesting there and others who came to find food on the broad lawn. They were small birds, wearing dark brown feathers on the upper parts of their bodies and lighter grayish ones underneath. Even their bills were marked in the same way, with the upper half dark and the lower half light. Their wings were short and blunt, and they had a habit of holding their tails well up in the air.

People said that Mrs. Wren was very fussy, and perhaps it was true, but even then she was not a cross person. Besides, if she wished to do a thing over five times in order to make it suit her, she certainly had a perfect right to do so. It was she who always chose the nesting-place and settled all the plans for the family. Mr. Wren was quite content to have it so, since that was the custom among Wrens, and it saved him much work. Mr. Wren was not lazy. He simply wanted to save time for singing, which he considered his own particular business. Besides, he never forgot what had happened to a cousin of his, a young fellow who found fault with his wife and insisted on changing to another nesting-place. It had ended in his going, and her staying there and marrying another Wren. So he had lost both his home and his wife by finding fault.

Now the April days had come, with their warm showers

and green growing grass. A pair of English Sparrows, who had nested in the woodbine the summer before and raised several large broods of bad-mannered children, decided that they would like to try living in the bird-house. Having been on the place all winter, they began work early. The Blackbirds were already back, and one reminded them that it belonged to the Wrens.

"Guess not now," said Mr. Sparrow, with a bad look in his eyes. "Nothing belongs to anybody else if I want it. Do you see?" Then he picked up and swallowed a fat Grub which the Blackbird had uncovered for himself and left lying there until he should finish talking. One could hardly blame the Blackbird for being vexed about this, for everybody knows that English Sparrows really prefer seeds, and that this one ate the Grub only to be mean. It did not make the Blackbird any happier to hear his relatives laugh at him in the evergreens above, and he made up his mind to get even with that Sparrow.

The Sparrows pitched all the old nest out of doors and began quarrelling with each other about building their own. They always quarrelled. Indeed, that was the way in which they had courted each other. Mrs. Sparrow had two lovers, and she married the one who would stand the worst pecking from her. "For," she said, "what is the use of having a husband unless you can beat him when you fight with him?"

Now they stuffed the dainty little bird-house full of straws, sticks, feathers, and anything they could find, until there was hardly room left in which to turn around. They were just beginning to wonder if they must throw some out when they heard the happy song of Mr. Wren.

"Get inside!" cried Mr. Sparrow to his wife. "I will stand on the porch and fight them."

Down flew Mr. and Mrs. Wren. "Oh, isn't it pleasant to get home again?" she exclaimed. "But what is that Sparrow doing on our porch?"

"This is our home now," said Mrs. Sparrow, "and we are very busy. Get out of my way."

"Your home?" cried the Wrens. "How is that? You lived in the woodbine last season and knew that this was ours. You are surely not in earnest."

Mr. Wren looked at his wife and she nodded. Then he flew at Mr. Sparrow and they fought back and forth on the grape trellis near by them, in the air, then on the ground. Mrs. Sparrow peeped out of the open door to see if her husband needed help. He was the larger of the two, but not so quick in darting and turning. Now they passed out of sight behind the tool-house and she forgot Mrs. Wren and flew down to see better. She was hardly off the tiny porch when Mrs. Wren darted in. Mrs. Sparrow saw when it was too late what a mistake she had made, and tried to get back. She reached the porch again just in time to have a lot of straws, twigs, and feathers poked into her face by the angry Mrs. Wren.

"I am cleaning house," said Mrs. Wren. "My house, too! Get out of my way!" Then she pushed out more of the same sort of stuff. Mrs. Sparrow tried to get in, and every time she put her head through the doorway she was pecked by Mrs. Wren. And she deserved it. She called Mr. Sparrow, but he could not help her, and Mr. Wren was so pleased that he sat on top of the tool-house and sang and sang and sang. To look at him you would have thought he was trying to kill himself. He puffed up his throat and swelled up his body and sang so fast that he seemed to be saying about four words at a time.

"Good for you! Good for you! Good for you!" he sang. "Stick to it! Stick to it! Stick to it! I'm here! I'm here! I'm here, here, here!"

Mrs. Wren was too busy to say much, but she did a great deal. Every scrap of the nest was thrown out, and as she worked she decided to keep that house if she starved there.

This was in the middle of the morning and she could not get out to feed until late in the afternoon. Mr. Wren found some delicious insects on the grapevines, and tried to carry a few billfuls to his wife, but the Sparrows prevented him. He would have enjoyed his own dinner better if she could have eaten with him. When he asked how she was, she chirped back that she was hungry but would not give up. Mr. Wren spent most of his time walking around the roof of the tool-house in circles, dragging his wings on the shingles, and saying, "Tr-r-r-r-r-r!" He was so angry that sometimes he could not say anything else. The Sparrows sat on the grape trellis and said mean things.

They were still doing this late in the afternoon, while the tree shadows grew longer and longer on the lawn with the lowering of the sun. Suddenly a Blackbird alighted on the trellis. It was the same one whose fat Grub Mr. Sparrow had stolen.

"This has gone far enough," said he. "This house belongs to the Wrens and they are going to have it. *I* say so. If I catch either of you Sparrows around here again, I will drive you

THE FIGHT FOR THE BIRD HOUSE.

off the place. I can do it, too. You may think it over until the next time that grapevine is blown against the tool-house. If you do not go then, there will be *trouble*." He ruffled up his feathers and glared with his yellow eyes. That was all he had to do. Before the grapevine swayed again, the Sparrows were far away.

The Wrens thanked him, even before Mrs. Wren ate her late dinner. "You are welcome," he said. "It was just fun for me. I cannot bear those Sparrows, and I hoped they would stay and give me a chance to fight them. How I wish they had stayed!" He looked sad and disappointed.

"I'll never have another such good chance," said he. And he never did. Perhaps it was just as well, although there are times when it is not wrong to fight, and the Wrens think this would have been one.

THE FIR-TREE NEIGHBORS

WITH so many trees in the yard, it always seemed a little strange that three families should choose to build so close together in one. Still, it must also be remembered that there were many birds who liked to build near the big house, and thought of that yard as home.

The Lady spoke of this tree as "The Evergreen Apartment House." The birds simply called it "The Tallest Fir Tree."

Early in the spring a pair of English Sparrows decided to build there. Perhaps one should say that Mrs. Sparrow decided, since her husband had nothing to say about it, except to murmur "Yes, dear," when she told him of her choice. They built well up in the tree, and had a big mass of hay, grass, and feathers together there when the Blackbirds came. This would have more than made a nest for most birds. Mrs. Sparrow called it only a beginning, and was always looking for more to add to it.

When the Blackbirds came in a dashing flock, they began hunting for building places and talking it all over among themselves. One mother Blackbird, who had nested on the place the year before, had counted on having that particular tree.

"I decided on it last fall," said she, "before I went South, and I have been planning for it all winter. I shall build in it just the same." She shut her bill in such a way that nobody could doubt her meaning exactly what she said. Her husband didn't like the place particularly well, but she said something to him which settled it. "You need not ruffle up your feathers for me," she said, "or stand on tip-toe to squeak at me, unless you are willing to live there."

They built higher than the nest of the English Sparrows. "We have always been well up in the world," she said, "and we do not care to come down now." That was all right. One could not blame them for feeling above the English Sparrows.

The English Sparrows had added more stuff to what they had, and the Blackbirds had their nest about half done when a pair of Hairbirds came to look for a comfortable tree. They were a young couple, just married that spring, and very devoted to each other. They did not decide matters in the same way as the English Sparrow, and the Blackbirds.

Although there were eleven other great evergreens in the yard, besides a number of trellises covered with vines, and all the vine-covered porches, there was no place which suited them so well as that particular tree. Yet each was so eager to please the other that it was rather hard to get either to say what he really thought. They perched on the tips of the fir branches and chattered and twittered all morning about it.

"What do you think?" Mrs. Hairbird said.

"What do you?" he replied.

"But I want to know what *you* think," she insisted.

"And I would rather know what *you* think," said he.

"No, but really," asked she, "do you like this tree?"

"Do you?" asked Mr. Hairbird.

"Yes, yes," answered she.

"So do I!" he said, with a happy twitter. "Isn't it queer how we always like the same things?"

"I wonder if we like the same branch?" said Mrs. Hairbird, after a long pause, in which both picked insects off the fir-tree and ate them.

"Which branch do you like?" asked he. But he could not help looking out of the side of his eye at the one he most fancied. He could not look out of the corner of his eye, you know, because round eyes have no corners, and being a bird his eyes were perfectly round.

"I like that one," she cried, and laughed to think how easily she had found out his choice. Then he laughed, too, and it was all decided, although Mrs. English Sparrow, fussing around in her mass of hay and feathers above them, declared that she never heard such silliness in her life, and that when she had made up her own mind that was enough. She never bothered her husband with questions. Mr. English Sparrow heard her say this, and thought he would rather like to be bothered in that way.

Mrs. Blackbird thought it all a great joke. "When they have been married as long as I have," she said, "it wont take so long to decide things." Mrs. Blackbird laughed at everything, but she was mistaken about this, for the Hairbirds, or Chipping Sparrows, as they are sometimes called, are always devoted and unselfish.

It being the custom in their family, the newcomers built quite low in the tree. Such a happy time as they had. Every bit of grass root which either of them dragged loose and brought to the tree, was the prettiest and stoutest and best they had ever seen. And when it got to the Horsehairs for lining, they visited all the barns for a block around, hunting for them. Once, when Mrs. Hairbird wished for a white hair for one particular place, Mr. Hairbird even watched for a white Horse, and pulled it out of his tail.

You can imagine how surprised the Horse was when he felt that little tweak at his tail, and, looking around, saw a small brown bird pulling at one of his longest hairs. "I am sorry to annoy you," said this bird, "but Mrs. Hairbird needed a white hair."

"That is all right," said the Horse, to whom one hair was a very small matter, and who dearly loved a joke. "Please tell Mrs. Hairbird that my tail is hers if she wishes it."

"Your tail is hers!" exclaimed Mr. Hairbird, who ought to have seen the joke, since he was not an English Sparrow. "Oh, no, surely not! Surely your tail is not her tail. They are quite different, you know!" Then he understood and hurried away, but not in time to help hearing the Horse laugh.

When the white hair was woven in, the nest was done, and Mrs. Hairbird laid in it four greenish blue eggs with dark brown specks. In the nest above were six greenish white ones with brown and light purple spots. In the nest above that were five dingy streaked and speckled ones. Mrs. Hairbird said that hers were by far the prettiest. "It is not because I laid them," she said to her husband. "It is not for that reason that I think so, but they really are."

Mr. and Mrs. Hairbird were the only ones who paid for the chance to build in the tree. They picked insects off the branches, insects that would have robbed the tree of some of its strength.

The Blackbirds would not bother with such small bits of food. The English Sparrows should have paid in the same way, but they would not.

Their great-great-great- —a great many times great- —grandparents were brought over to this country just to eat the insects which were hurting the trees and shrubs, but when they got here they would not do it. "No, indeed," said they; "we are here now, and we will eat what we choose." Their great-great-great- —a great many times great- —grandchildren were just like them.

Silvertip often came to sit under this tree. He called it a family tree, because it had so many little families in its branches. He could not climb it. The fine branches and twigs were so close together that he could not get up the trunk, and they were not strong enough for him to step from one to another of them.

As might perhaps have been expected, there was some gossiping among neighbors in this tree. The Blackbirds usually climbed to their nest by beginning at the bottom of the trunk and going around and around it to the top. This took them so close to the other nests that they could not help looking in. At any rate, they didn't help it.

Mrs. Blackbird told Mrs. Hairbird that the way Mrs. Sparrow kept house was a disgrace to the tree. Mrs. Sparrow told her to be very careful not to leave her eggs or young children alone when the Blackbirds were around, because when they were very hungry they had been known to—! She did not finish her sentence in words, but just ruffled up her feathers and fluttered her wings, which was a great deal meaner. If she were going to say such things about people, you know, she should have said them, and not made Mrs. Hairbird guess the worst part.

Mr. Blackbird said he pitied Mr. Sparrow with all his heart. He knew something what it was to have a wife try to run things, but that if Mrs. Blackbird had ever acted as Mrs. Sparrow did, he would leave her, even if it were in the early spring.

Mr. Sparrow said it was most disagreeable to have such noisy neighbors as the Blackbirds overhead. That if his wife had known they were coming to that tree, she would have chosen another place. "Of course it was too late for her to change when she found it out," he said. "Her nest was well begun, and she had some very choice straws and feathers which she didn't care to move. You know how such things get spoiled in carrying them from place to place."

Most of these things were told to Mrs. Hairbird, because she was at home with the eggs, but she repeated them all to her husband when he came. She even told him how Mr. Sparrow flew down one day just after a quarrel with his wife, and of all the things he had said when angry. It was quite right in Mrs. Hairbird to tell her husband, and yet she never chirped them to another bird. And that also was right.

When people talked these things to her, she always looked bright and pleasant, but she did not talk about them herself. Indeed, she often made excuses for her neighbors when she repeated things to her husband. For instance, when she told what Mrs. Sparrow had said about Mrs. Blackbird, she added: "I suppose that may be so, still I feel sure that

Mrs. Blackbird would not eat any of our children unless she were *dreadfully* hungry."

You can see what a sweet and wise little person Mrs. Hairbird was, and her husband was exactly like her. No matter how other people quarrelled, they did not. No matter what gossip they heard, they did not repeat it. And it ended just as such things always do.

In late spring, about the time that the Bees were gathering varnish for their homes, and every fir-tree tip had one or two buzzing around it, there was a dreadful quarrel in the family tree. Mrs. Sparrow wanted some grasses from the outside of the Blackbirds' nest, and she sat on her own and looked at them until she felt she could not live without them. Of course, that was very wrong. She might have forgotten all about them if she had made herself think about something else. Any bird who wants something he ought not to have should do that. She might better have looked down at her own breast, or counted her wing feathers over and over. However, she didn't. She took those grasses.

Mrs. Blackbird missed them, and then saw them woven loosely into the nest below hers. She did not say much, and she did not eat the eggs out of the Sparrows' nest. Some people said that she ate them, but that was a mistake. All that she did was to sit very quietly on her nest while a Red Squirrel ate them. When this same fellow would have eaten those in the nest below, both the Hairbirds being away, she drove him off herself.

You can imagine what the Sparrows said when they returned. Or perhaps you might better not try to, for they said very cross things. Then Mrs. Blackbird told what she thought about those stolen grasses, and her husband joined in, until there was more noise than a flock of Crows would make.

It ended in Mr. and Mrs. Sparrow tearing down that nest and building another in the woodbine, where most of their relatives lived. Some of their neighbors thought the Blackbirds right and some thought the Sparrows right, but through it all Mr. and Mrs. Hairbird were happy and contented, and brought up their four charming children to be as good birds as they were themselves.

The Sparrows often said that the worst thing about going away from the family tree was leaving the Hairbirds, who were such delightful neighbors. The Blackbirds said that the pleasantest thing about the tree was having the Hairbirds for neighbors. The Hairbirds were liked by everybody, and never made trouble between friends. It was all because they knew how and when to keep their bills shut.

A RED SQUIRREL ATE THEM.

THE INDUSTRIOUS FLICKERS

I F the Bad Boy who lived in the next block had known more about the habits of Flickers, there would probably have been no young ones to feed on the lawn of the big house. He had watched Mr. and Mrs. Flicker in the spring when they were making their nest ready, and had waited only long enough for the eggs to be laid before climbing the tall Lombardy poplar to rob it.

You must not think that Mr. and Mrs. Flicker were stupid in showing the Bad Boy where their nest was. There was never a more careful couple, but they were so large and handsome that, if they went anywhere at all, they were sure to be seen. After they had once been seen, it was easy for any one with plenty of time to watch and follow them home.

Mr. Flicker was clad mostly in golden brown, barred with black. He had a very showy black spot on his breast, which was just the shape of a new moon, black patches on his cheeks and smaller ones on his belly. The linings of his wings, and the quills of his long wing- and tail-feathers were a bright yellow, and on the back of his head he had a beautiful red band. All these were very fine, but the most surprising thing was a large patch of pure white feathers on the lower part of his back. These did not show except when he was flying. At other times his folded wings quite hid them from sight. Mrs. Flicker looked so much like her husband that you could not tell one from the other, unless you were near enough to see their cheeks. Then you would know, for Mrs. Flicker had no black spots on hers.

When the Bad Boy was sure that the nest was high up in the trunk of the old Lombardy poplar, just across the street from the big house, he waited until his mother and his big sister were out of the way, and then he climbed that tree and took the six white eggs out of it. That was a very, very cruel thing to do. It would have been bad enough to take one, but to take all six was a great deal worse. You will not pity the Bad Boy when you know that he tore his trousers and hurt one hand on his way down.

Poor Mrs. Flicker cried herself to sleep that night. "If we had not been careful," she sobbed, "I wouldn't feel so badly, but to have it happen after all the trouble we took! I am sure that when we cut the hole for our nest, not a single chip fell to the ground below. We carried them all far away before dropping them.

"Excepting the ones we left for the eggs to lie on," added Mr. Flicker, who was always particular and exact in what he said, even when in great trouble.

"Yes, excepting those," sobbed his poor wife. "I left a few of the best ones inside."

"I wonder where the eggs are now," said Mr. Flicker. He looked toward the Bad Boy's home as he spoke. If he had but known it, the Bad Boy had not one left. Two had been broken in coming down the tree (for his mouth had

A VERY CRUEL THING TO DO.

not been big enough to carry all six), three he had traded for marbles, and the last one, which he meant to keep for a "specimen," had rolled off his desk in school and smashed on the floor. The Bad Boy had been kept in at recess for this, but that did not make the egg whole again.

The Flickers went sadly to sleep, and dreamed of a land where Birds were as big as Cows and Boys as small as Goldfinches—where boys were afraid of birds and hid when they saw them coming.

When the morning sunshine awakened them and they had breakfasted well, Mrs. Flicker began to feel more hopeful. "I am really ashamed of myself," she said, "for being so discouraged. There would be some excuse for it if I were another kind of bird, but since I am a Flicker and can lay more eggs whenever my nest is robbed, I think I'd better stop crying and plan for six more."

"My brave wife!" exclaimed Mr. Flicker. "You are quite right. It is all very sad, but we will make the best of it and try to be happy."

The Bad Boy passed under the tree more than twenty times before the second lot of eggs were hatched, and he wished and wished for a Flicker's egg (only he called them High Holes, because they built in high holes). He never guessed that in the nest above his head lay six more just as fine as the ones he had stolen. It is not strange that he did not, for who but a Flicker can lay and lay and lay eggs when her nest is robbed?

Now the young Flickers were hatched and ready to leave their comfortable home. They were much more helpless than most young birds are when they leave the nest.

In fact, they could hardly fly at all, and had to tumble and sprawl their way to the ground, catching here and there in the branches of the poplar. Her neighbors thought Mrs. Flicker quite heartless to let them go so soon, but when she told them what a care her six nestlings were, they felt differently about it.

"Did you ever hear of such a thing?" exclaimed Mrs. Catbird, who thought herself quite overworked in caring for her six, and who had only known Flickers by sight before this. "Did you ever hear of such a thing? She tells me that she and Mr. Flicker not only have to find all the food for their children, but have to eat it for them also. I remember the Mourning Doves doing that, but then, they never have more than two children at a time, so it is not so hard."

"What is that?" asked a Blackbird, who, like the rest of her family, always wanted to know about everything.

"Why," repeated Mrs. Catbird, "the Flickers have to eat all the food they get for their children, and then, when it has become soft and ready for young birds, they unswallow it into their children's bills. It takes so much time to do this and to fly back and forth that they want to have them out of the nest as soon as possible. Then they can take them around with them."

You can imagine how anxious the parents were for a few days, while their six babies were still so awkward and helpless. They took them across the street to the lawn around the big house, and tucked them away in dusky places where their brown feathers would not show against anything light. Most of them were under the edge of a board walk, one was under a porch, and one was under a low branching evergreen. Mrs. Robin, who was then hatching her second brood, kept watch for Silvertip, and this was a great help to the Flickers on the ground below.

First one and then another of the young Flickers went out with one of the parents, and it was most interesting to see them fed. The Flickers, you know, are woodpeckers, and their long bills are slender, curved, and pointed, just right for picking Grubs and nice fat little Bugs out of tree-bark. Their tails, also, are stiff and right to prop them as they work up and around the trunk of a tree. Still, they feed on the ground more than on trees, and like Ants better than anything else in the world.

Now, one could see Mr. Flicker by an Ant-hill with a nestling beside him, his head going up and down like a hammer, and an Ant picked up in his bill at every stroke. Every now and then he would stop, turn his head, place his bill in that of his child, and unswallow some Ants, which the nestling would gulp down. Between feedings the nestling would settle his head between his shoulders, and slide his thin eyelids over his eyes. He never slid his thick eyelids over. He saved those for night, when he would really sleep.

While the father was feeding one, the mother would be feeding another. When these two were satisfied they were sent back to their hiding-places and two more had their turns. It was very hard work, in spite of their being so good. They never fussed or teased. They waited patiently for their turns and found no fault with the food.

"Oh," said Mrs. Flicker to her husband, as she swallowed the six hundred-and-forty-eighth Ant since sunrise. "I am so tired that I feel like giving up. If it were not for you and the children, I believe I would just as soon let that Cat catch me as not."

"I know," he answered. "I am very tired myself, and I am sure you must be more so. You do not seem strong since you were shut in so long while brooding the eggs."

"It is easier in one way, now that all are out of the nest," said she. "It saves my wings a great deal, but my neck and throat ache from such steady work. I used to rather enjoy eating for myself. The food tasted good, and it was something pleasant to do. This eating for a whole family is quite different."

"Well, it won't last much longer," her husband said comfortingly. "The children will soon be able to feed themselves, and you can have a good rest. Then we will go picnicking in the fields beyond this place, and every one shall get his own lunch."

In a few more days they did this, and for three mornings they might have been seen, in a happy party of eight, walking around together, quite as Pigeons do. At the end of the third day, Mr. Flicker said to his wife: "Well, my dear, are you having a good time? This is a pleasant change from caring for the children, isn't it?"

To his surprise, she turned her head away and did not answer. When he repeated his questions, she replied with a little choke in her voice. "It is very easy," she said, "and a great rest, but it seems to me I have nothing to do. I eat all I can and try to swallow slowly, but when my stomach is full I have to just walk around. I miss the children putting their dear little bills up to mine and taking food from me. I believe I am lonely."

Poor Mr. Flicker was young and inexperienced. He did not know how quickly some people change their minds, or how mothers miss the care of children.

"Isn't there something you can do," he asked, "to make you happier?"

"Could you help me clean out our old hole in the Lombardy poplar?" said she. "I believe I will lay some more eggs."

"What?" cried her husband. "When you have been so tired? And then you will be shut in so long while brooding them. Why not fly off on a pleasure trip with me?"

"I will," said she. "I'd love to go. But let us get the nest all ready first."

Mr. Flicker was young and inexperienced, as has been said before, yet he flew right off to work on that nest and let his wife do exactly as she chose. Which shows that, although she did change her mind and he could not understand why, they were a very happy and sensible couple, after all.

PLUCKY MRS. POLISTES

MRS. Polistes was a charming little widow, who had slept through the long, cold winter, snugly tucked away in a crack in the barn belonging to the big house. She had married late in the fall, but her husband was a lazy fellow who had soon left her, and sat around in the sunshine with his brothers and the other fellows whom he knew. Each sat in his own little spot, and at last died because he was so lazy. That is the way with many insects who will not work. They die, and the members of their families who keep busy live to a good old age.

Now it was spring, and Mrs. Polistes awakened happy and full of plans. You must not think her hard-hearted to be happy after her husband was dead. If he had been a different sort of a fellow, you know, she would have missed him more. As it was, she did not even think of marrying again, but set to work to build her home and bring up her children to be good and industrious Wasps like herself.

She asked another young widow to work with her, and together they flew around hunting for a good building-place. They talked first of hanging their nest from the branch of a bush, but both were very careful Wasps and preferred to be sheltered from rain-storms. (Some of their family, however, did choose to build on bushes). Next they flew into the ice-house and tried several of the corners there. Mrs. Polistes did most of the talking, being a Wasp of very decided opinions.

"It is too chilly here," she said. "I should never feel like myself in such a cold place. And you know perfectly well," she added, "that if anybody should disturb us in here, we would not be warm enough to sting. Or if we did sting, we could never pump much poison in."

There was nothing to be said after that, for everybody knows that unless a Wasp can sting, and sting hard, he is not safe.

Then they looked at the porch ceilings. Their cousins, the Vespæ, had started some nests there, and they preferred not to be too near them. The Vespæ were very good Wasps, but, as Mrs. Polistes said, "We wish to bring our children up to be Polistes Wasps, and if they see the way in which the Vespæ live, they will get their ideas all mixed. I do not think it wise to rear them within sight of covered nests, and you know as well as I [this was to her friend] how the Vespæ wall around their cells."

After this they found what they thought a most delight-ful place. It was just inside the closed shutters of a bedroom window. The upper sash of the window was lowered, and inside of that was a fine wire netting. "Excellent!" said the friend. "That is probably there to keep the people inside from coming out this way."

Mrs. Polistes was not quite sure that the netting was there for that reason, but she liked the place, so they flew off together to the stump-fence which enclosed the great field back of the house. Then they looked for an old stump, sat down on one of its prongs, and began to gnaw off wood fibre. They did not talk much, for they had to work so hard with their mouths. Each gnawed length-wise of the grain until she had a little bundle of wood fibre in her jaws. When these were ready, they flew off to their chosen spot and began to build. First it had to be chewed for a long time, until it was soft and pulpy, then, working together and very carefully, they built a slender, stemlike thing down from the top of the window casing.

It took many trips to bring enough wood fibre for this, and between trips they had to stop for food. It took longer to find it so early in the season than it would later, for Flies and insects of all kinds were scarce and there were not many flowers yet. Some of those which looked most tempting were for Bees, and not for Wasps. The Wasps, you know, have such short tongues that they cannot get the honey from most flowers. That is why they so like the flat-topped ones and the shallow ones into which they can reach easily. Mrs. Polistes and her friend at last found a bed of sweet clover which made them fine meals.

That first day they only chose the place for their home and got the stem ready, but it was not long before they had three tiny cells begun and eggs in two of them. Mrs. Polistes and the homemakers of her family always insisted upon doing in this way.

"It not only saves time," said Mrs. Polistes, "to have several kinds of work going at once, but it rests one, too. When my jaws are tired of chewing wood fibre or shaping it into cells, I rest myself by laying an egg. And when my sting is tired from that, I hunt food for myself and the babies. There is nothing like having a change of work."

Mrs. Polistes spoke in this way about her sting, you understand, because it was her ovipositor, or egg-layer, as well. She really used it in this way much more than the other. She did not wish to sting with it any more than she had to. It tired her very much to pump poison through it when she stung. There was always the danger, too, if she stung a large creature, like a boy, of getting it stuck in him and not being able to pull it out without breaking. If it broke, she would die.

Mrs. Polistes and her friends took turns in laying eggs, and soon had to begin another row of cells around the first. They laid their oblong white eggs in them long before the cells were done, and had to stick them up to the side walls to keep them from falling out of the opening at the bottom. Then, when they had time, they lowered the walls of the cells. When the babies hatched, which was only a few days after the laying of the eggs, they brought food and fed them as they hung in their cells.

The Lady who lived in the big house watched this very often, and Mrs. Polistes and her friend became so used to it that they were not at all frightened or disturbed. Wasps, you know, are very easily tamed by any one who moves gently. The Lady stood on a chair just inside the window, and put her face close to the screen. She could see exactly how the mother Wasps bit the cell walls into shape, moving backward all the time. She could see Mrs. Polistes and her friend bring nicely chewed-up Flies and other insects with which to feed the babies, and watched them go quietly from cell to cell, giving a lunch to each.

They were very interesting babies. Being still fastened to the cell wall by the tail end, only their heads showed, tiny white heads with two little eyes and brown, horny jaws. Sometimes, when Mrs. Polistes and her friend were away, the Lady would softly lower the screen from the top of the window and touch the nest very, very gently with her pencil. Then each baby thought it was his mother or his aunt, and thrust his tiny head out for food. Perhaps this was not kind to the Wasp babies, but if the Lady made them and their mother amuse her, she was also very careful about worrying them. The older Wasps never found out that the screen had been moved, and the Lady told everybody in the house that the upper window sash must not be put up. She feared that it would strike the outer cells and loosen the nest if raised.

All would have gone well if it had not been for that dreadful thunderstorm just before daylight one morning. The Gentleman found the raindrops blowing in through the bedroom window, and got it almost closed before he remembered the Wasps' nest. Then he lowered the upper sash again and left it down, in spite of the rain.

Sad to say, when morning came the dainty little nest lay on the top edge of the upper sash. It had been loosened but not crushed, and had fallen on to the only place it could. Mrs. Polistes and her friend were flying in and out with food for the babies, who were now all tilted up sidewise, instead of hanging head downward, as Wasp babies should.

"I don't understand it at all," said the friend. "Everything is exactly as it was when we went to sleep, except that the nest has fallen."

"I was dreaming as I hung on the nest last night," replied

Mrs. Polistes, "when suddenly I felt a great jar and was knocked off."

"So was I," exclaimed her friend.

"I flew around in the dark until I found it again," added Mrs. Polistes, "but I had to wait until daylight to see what had happened. Oh, dear! It is so upsetting to find one's home upside down, and two of my children are just ready to spin their cocoons."

"Your children?" asked her friends quite sharply, for it made her cross to have such misfortunes. "Your children? One of those children is mine."

"Which one?" asked Mrs. Polistes, who thought she remembered her own egg-laying.

"I don't know which, now that the nest is all turned around," was the answer. "It has mixed those babies up, and I can't pick out mine."

"Well, it doesn't really matter," said Mrs. Polistes kindly. "You may call them both yours, if you want to. Just laying the egg doesn't count for much, and we have both fed and cared for them. I supposed we would share babies as we have shared everything else."

This made the friend ashamed of herself, and she said that she was sorry she was cross, and that Mrs. Polistes should call one of the cocoons hers.

Then they put their heads together to decide what to do with the nest. When Wasps put their heads together, they stroke each other with their long feelers, or antennæ, and in that way each is sure what the other is thinking. They also smell with these feelers, you know, and some people say that they hear with them. A Wasp with broken antennæ can do but little, and as for not having any—why, a Wasp might as well die at once as to lose his antennæ.

Poor Mrs. Polistes and her little friend! It looked now as though if they were to bring up those children at all, they would have to do it wrong side up. The right way, you know, is to raise them upside down, and here they were lying with their heads up in cells that were open at the top.

Yet, even while they were thinking about it, something else happened. The window sash on which the nest lay began to move slowly and steadily upward, not stopping until the nest almost touched the casing above.

Mrs. Polistes was so frightened! She thought that nest, children, and all were about to be crushed flat. She said afterward that she was so scared she could think of nothing but stinging, and there was nobody whom she could sting. Of course, that would be so, for a Wasp who is frightened always wants to sting, and it is a great comfort to him if he can. It gives him something new to think about, you know.

The Lady was the one who slowly pushed the sash upward. She thought it might help the poor little mothers somewhat. And it did. They began at once to hunt food for their children and bring it in. The nest now lay on the middle of the sash. Before it was knocked loose, it had hung over in one corner of the casing. It would now have been much nearer for the little mothers to crawl through the middle of the shutters. But they were Wasps, and Wasps do not easily change their paths, so they entered each time at precisely the old place, and then flew or crawled to the nest. One who watches Wasps in the open air would never expect them to go by a roundabout way, for they fly so swiftly, strongly, and directly, yet they are easily puzzled by changes around the nest.

Mrs. Polistes had not fed more than half her share of children when she had an idea. She struck her antennæ against those of her friend and told her about it. Then they walked all around the nest, looked at it, felt of it, and gave it little pushes. The Lady stood on her chair watching them, but they were used to her and did not mind it.

"I believe we can," said Mrs. Polistes.

"It would be lovely if we could," answered her friend, "but I am sure we can't."

"We can try it, anyway," said Mrs. Polistes.

"What is the use?" said her friend. "It will just scare the babies and tire us out. We might better feed them where they are."

"No," said Mrs. Polistes, and she spoke very positively. "No! There are worse things than being scared, and they must stand it. If we leave this nest as it is, the first hard wind will tumble it around, and a rolling nest raises no Wasps."

"Mothers!" cried the children, in their weak little voices. "Mothers! What are you talking about?"

"We are going to fix your nest up again," answered Mrs. Polistes. "Now be good children, and do not bother us with questions."

Then she and her friend began pushing and pulling and rolling and tumbling the nest around to get it more nearly right side up. They got it tipped so that all the cells slanted downward, and then they began chewing wood-pulp and building a new stem toward it from the casing above. Mrs. Polistes worked so hard that her friend was really worried about her. She would not take time to eat. At last her friend stood right in front of her and unswallowed a drop of delicious honey. "You must eat it," she said. "When I swallowed it, I meant to keep it for myself, but I would much rather give it to you." Mrs. Polistes lapped it up and felt stronger at once.

Such a stout stem as this one was! The cell walls also had to be strengthened with more of the wood pulp and sticky saliva from the Wasps' mouths, because the stem was to be fastened to them in a new place. It was not until the next day that all this work was done, and the mothers could begin living in the old way again. The babies were glad when this time came, for they had not been fed so much while extra building had to be done.

The two children who were ready to do so had spun their cocoons in their cells. They used the silky stuff which they had in their mouths, and which oozed out through a little hole in each child's lip. The others were growing finely, the nest was hanging from its new stem, the Lady had lowered the window sash once more, and Mrs. Polistes and her friend had a little time to rest. "I am going to give myself a thorough cleaning," said she, licking her front feet off and then rubbing her head with them. "And then I am going away for a playspell."

She cleaned herself all over with her legs, and was most particular about her antennæ. She had special cleaners for these, you know—little prongs which grow in the bend of the fourth and fifth joints of the forelegs and fit closely around the antennæ, scraping them clean between the bent legs and the prongs. You can see she would need to be particular, because she had to do her talking, her smelling, part of her feeling, and perhaps some of her hearing with them. When she was well scrubbed, she took a good look at the children and flew off for a fine time, while her friend took care of things at home.

Such fun as she had! She caught and ate Cabbage Butterflies, Earwigs, and other food which will not be touched by most insects and birds. She supped a tiny bit of honey from the sweet clover, and then flew straight to the cherry tree. A Catbird was already there, helping himself to the best in the tree-top, and laughing at the Lady when she tried to scare him away. He was never afraid of her throwing straight enough to hit him.

Mrs. Polistes sipped juice from one ripe cherry after another, and then, sad to say, she began to drink from one which was over-ripe. She may not have known that it was so, but not knowing made no difference with her feelings. She was soon so weak in all her six legs that she could not walk, and so weak in her wings that her big front and her small hind pairs would not stay hooked together as they should be. It was a long time before she could get home.

When she *did* go, she carried back some good things for the children, and then took care of them while her friend had a playspell. After all, when she was once rested, she enjoyed work better than play. Her children all grew finely, and so did those of her friend, which was exceedingly fortunate. If one had died, you know, after the tumbling down of the nest, each would have thought it her own.

The little Wasps also grew up as well as could be expected. The sons all took after their father, and were lazy, but, apart from that, they were all right. The Queen daughters were exactly like their mothers, and the little Workers, of whom there were the most of all, were the greatest of comforts. They did the work of the home as soon as they were old enough. It was truly a family which paid for saving.

When people asked Mrs. Polistes how she ever came to think of such a thing as putting the nest up again, she simply flirted her wings and replied: "Where else should I put it? I couldn't leave my children there."

SILVERTIP STOPS A QUARREL

THIS is the story of something which did not really happen in the dooryard of the big house, yet it has seemed best to put it in with these tales because it could all be seen from that yard, and because Silvertip had a part in it.

He was sitting quietly upon the broad top-rail of the fence one afternoon, wishing that the sun would shine again. It had rained most of the time for three days, and he did not like wet weather. He thought it was going to clear off, for the clouds had not sent any drops down since noon. The grass and walks were still damp, so he sat on the fence-rail. He had stayed in the house so long that he was tired of it, and he was also watching a pair of Robins who had built a nest on one of the up-stairs window-ledges. They had put it right on top of a last year's Robins' nest, and that was on one of the year before. You can see that it was well worth looking at.

Silvertip had been here only a short time, when he saw Mr. White Cat, from another house, walking over to the one across the street. Miss Tabby Cat lived there, and he knew that Mr. Tiger Cat was around somewhere. Mr. White Cat looked very cross. He was one of those people who are good-natured only when the sun is shining and they have everything they want, and this, you know, is not the best sort of a person.

"Um-hum!" said Silvertip to himself. "I think there will be a fight before long. I will watch." He stood up and stretched himself carefully and sat down the other way, so as to see all that happened. Silvertip himself never fought. He spent a great deal of time in making believe fight, and usually entertained his Cat callers by glaring, spitting, or even growling at them, but he never really clawed and scratched and bit. He did not care to have sore places all over him, and he did not wish to get his ears chewed off.

"I can get what I want without fighting for it, so why should I fight?" said he. He was a very good sort of Cat, and had never been really cross about anything except when the Little Boy came to live in the big house. Then he had been sulky for weeks, and would not stay in the room with the Little Boy at all. He thought that if he made enough fuss about it, the Gentleman and the Lady would not let the Little Boy live there. When he found the Little Boy would stay anyway, he stopped being cross. After a while he loved him too.

No, Silvertip would not fight. But he very much liked to watch other Cats fight. Now he saw Miss Tabby sit quietly by the house across the street and right in front of a hole under the porch. She had her legs tucked beneath her, and her tail neatly folded around them. She looked as though she had found a small spot which was dry, and wanted to get all of herself on that.

Just inside the open doorway of the barn, there sat Mr.

Tiger Cat. He also had his legs tucked in and his tail folded around him. Mr. White Cat walked straight up to him and stood stiff-legged. Mr. Tiger Cat, who had just eaten a hearty meal and wanted an after-dinner nap, half opened his eyes and looked at him. Then he closed them again.

This made Mr. White Cat more ill natured still. He did not like to have people look at him and then shut their eyes. He began to switch his tail and stand his hair on end. He decided to make the other Cat fight anyway. He cared all the more about it because Miss Tabby was watching him. He had not noticed Silvertip. "Er-oo!" said he, drawing back his head and lowering his tail stiffly. "Did you say it was going to rain, or did you say it was not?"

"I hardly think it will," answered Mr. Tiger Cat pleasantly.

"You don't think it will, hey?" asked Mr. White Cat. "Well, I say it will pour."

Mr. Tiger Cat slid his thin eyelids over his eyes.

"Did you hear me?" asked Mr. White Cat, still standing in the same way.

"Certainly," answered the other.

"Well, what do you say to that?" asked Mr. White Cat, and now he began to stand straighter and hold his tail out behind.

"I am willing it should pour," said Mr. Tiger Cat, beginning to uncover his eyes slowly.

"Oo-oo! You are?" growled Mr. White Cat. "You are, are you? Well, I am not!"

There was no answer. You see Mr. Tiger Cat did not want to fight. He did not need to just then, and he never fought for the fun of it when his stomach was so full. He supposed he would have to in the end, for he knew when a fellow has really made up his mind to it, and is picking a quarrel, it has to end in that way. At least, it has to end in that way when one is a Cat. If one is bigger and better, there are other ways of ending it.

Mr. Tiger Cat knew all this, and yet he waited. "The longer I wait," he thought, "the more I shall feel like it. My stomach will not be so full and I can fight better. He needn't think he can come around and pick a quarrel and chew my ears when Miss Tabby is looking on. No indeed."

You see Mr. Tiger Cat was also fond of Miss Tabby.

"Er-roo!" said Mr. White Cat, straightening his legs until he stood very tall indeed. "Er-roo!"

He had made himself so angry now that he could not talk in words at all. Mr. Tiger Cat sat still.

"Er-row!" said Mr. White Cat, speaking way down his throat. "Er-row!" Mr. Tiger Cat sat still.

Silvertip became so excited that he could not stay longer on the fence. He dearly loved to see a good fight, you know, so he jumped quietly down without looking away from the barn door, and began walking softly toward it. He knew that when a Cat got to saying "Er-row!" down in his throat, something was going to happen very soon. Silvertip did not know, however, exactly what it would be because he did not see a couple of big Dogs trotting down the street toward him.

He crept nearer and nearer to the barn, hardly looking where he stepped for fear of missing some of the fun. His pretty white paws got wet and dirty, but that did not matter now. Paws could be licked clean at any time. Fights must be watched while they may be found.

"Ra-ow!" said Mr. White Cat, giving a forward jump.

"Pht!" answered Mr. Tiger Cat, standing stiffly on his hind feet and letting his front ones hang straight down. He was wide awake now, and ready to teach Mr. White Cat a lesson in politeness.

"Bow-wow!" said the Dogs just behind Silvertip. He might have run up a tree near by, but he had a bright idea.

"I'll do it," he exclaimed. "The Little Boy says it is wicked to fight, anyway." Then he ran straight in through that open door and jumped to a high shelf in the barn. He saw Miss Tabby turn a summersault backward and crawl under the porch.

Mr. Tiger Cat took a long jump to the sill of a high window. Mr. White Cat did not seem to care at all whether it was going to pour or not. He sprang to the top round of a ladder. The Dogs frisked below, wagging their tails and talking to each other about the Cats.

Mr. Tiger Cat, who was very well-bred and could always think of something polite to say, remarked to Silvertip: "Your call was quite an unexpected pleasure!" He had a smiling look around the mouth as he spoke.

"Yes," answered Silvertip, who liked a joke as well as anybody, unless it were a joke on himself alone. "Yes, I found myself coming this way, and just ran in."

Then they both settled down comfortably where they were, tucking their feet under them and wrapping their tails around. Nobody said anything to Mr. White Cat, who had no chance to sit down, and, indeed, could hardly keep from falling off the ladder.

The Dogs frisked and tumbled in the barn for a while

and hung around the foot of the ladder. They knew they could not get either of the others, but they had a happy hope that Mr. White Cat might fall.

When at last the Dogs had gone, and Mr. White Cat had also sneaked away, Mr. Tiger Cat said: "Fighting is very wrong."

"Yes," replied Silvertip, "very wrong indeed. But," he added, "I'll make believe fight anybody." So he jumped stiffly down and Mr. Tiger Cat jumped stiffly down, and they glared and growled at each other all the afternoon and never bit or even unsheathed a claw. They had a most delightful time, and Miss Tabby came out from under the porch and smiled on them both. She loved Cats who acted bravely.

A YOUNG SWIFT TUMBLES

In one of the chimneys of the big house several families of Chimney Swifts had built their homes. They had come north in April and flown straight to this particular place. It was the family home of this branch of the Swifts, and every year since great-grandfather Swift discovered it, some of his children and grandchildren had come back there to build. They were quite airy, and thought a great deal about appearances. "Swifts are sure to be judged by the chimney in which they live," they said, "and there is no use in choosing a poor one when there are good ones to be found."

Nobody would have dared remind these Chimney Swifts that their great-great-great-great-grandparents lived in hollow trees, if indeed any of their friends knew it. They themselves never spoke of the Swifts who still do so, and since they had always lived in a land of chimneys, they did not dream of the times when there were none to be found. Of course, before the white men came to this country Swifts had to build in hollow trees.

You can just imagine what a happy, busy place this chimney was in the springtime, when last year's nests were being torn down and new ones were building. The older Swifts

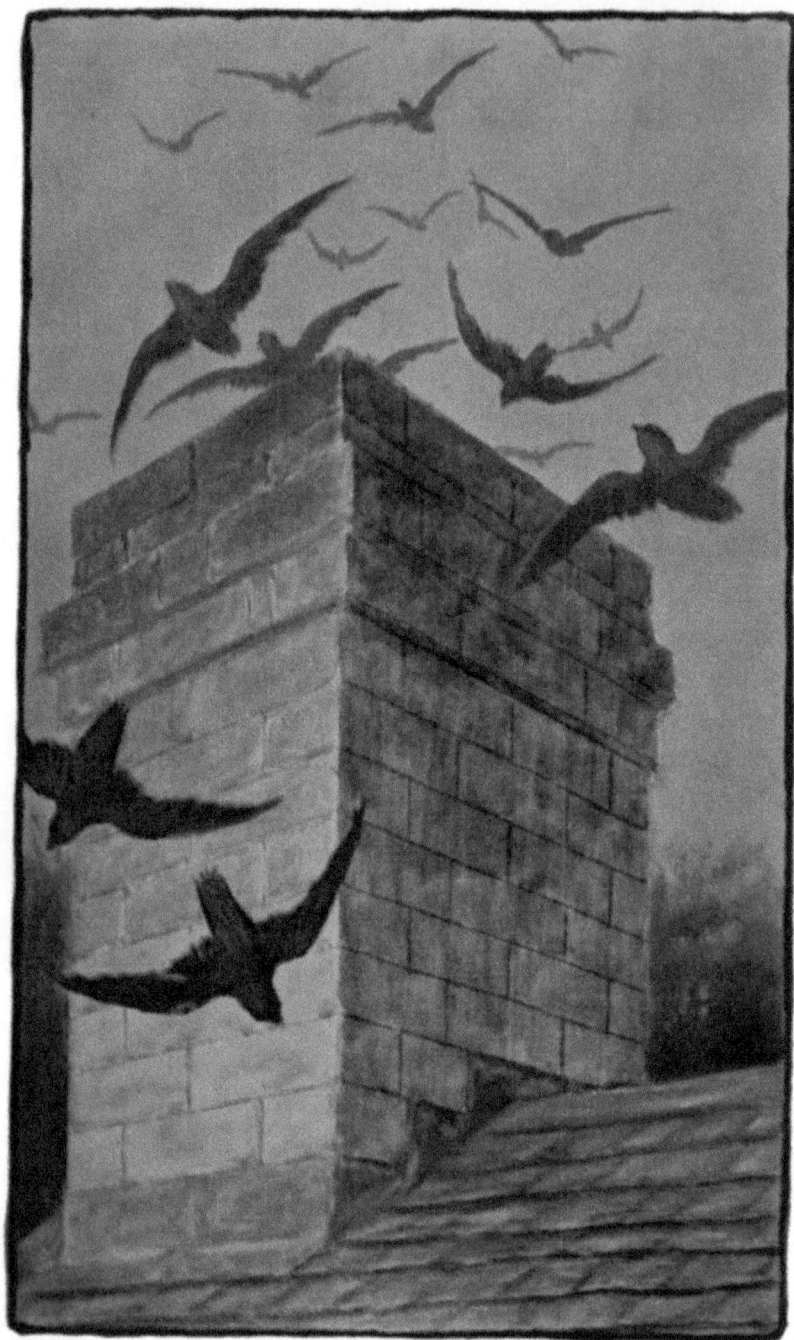

THE CHIMNEY-SWIFT'S HOME.

were there and those who were to keep house for the first time. Then, of course, the younger ones had married and brought new wives there, and they had to be introduced and shown all over the chimney.

Some wanted to build nearer the top than others, and the older ones were always advising the younger ones. It was so hard for a Swift mother to remember that her married son was old enough to decide things for himself; and many such mothers fluttered around the sons' nests, telling them how to place each twig, and giving the new wives advice as to how to bring up the babies who would soon come to live with them.

This story is about a young couple who built the lowest nest of all. They were dressed just alike in sleek, sooty, brown feathers, which were of a lighter shade on their throats. Their necks and heads were very broad, their bills short but able to open very wide; their wings were longer than their tails, and the quills of their tail feathers stuck out stiff and bare far beyond the soft, feathery part. The Swifts are all very proud of these bare quills. "There are not many birds," they say, "who can show their quills in that fashion."

These quills are very useful, too, for after a Swift has broken off a tiny twig for his nest, he has to cling to the side of the chimney and fix it into place, and he could not do this without supporting himself by these tail quills. It is hard work building nests, and you can see that it would be. They have to cling with both feet, support themselves with their tails, put each tiny twig in place with their bills, and glue it there with sticky saliva from their mouths or else with tree-gum.

The young husband who was building his first home low down in the chimney was a sturdy and rather wilful fellow, who was very sure what he wanted, and just as sure that he was going to get it. When he said, "I shall do this," or, "I am going to have that," other people had learned to keep still. They sometimes had a smiling look around the bill, but they said nothing. His wife was a sweet and sensible Swift who never made a fuss about anything, or bragged of what she meant to do. Still, other Swifts who watched them said that she had her way quite as often as he had his.

It was really she who had chosen to build well down in the chimney. Her husband had preferred to be near the top, and she had agreed to that, but spoke of what would happen if one of their children should fall out of the nest.

"There is no need of one falling out," said Mr. Swift. "Tell them to lie still and not push around. Then they will not fall out."

Mrs. Swift fixed one of the feathers on the under side of her left wing, and then remarked: "And you do not think it would disturb you to have our neighbors passing all the time."

"Yes, I do," he replied. "I have thought so from the first, and I am thinking that it might be well to build lower for that reason. Then we could be passing the others instead."

He flew down and pecked at the bricks in a few places to make sure that he could fasten a nest securely. Then he came back to his wife. "I have decided to build the lowest nest of all," said he, "but you understand it is not on account of the children. There is no sense in their moving around in the nest."

"I understand," said Mrs. Swift, and he flew away for twigs while she stayed behind to visit with her mother-in-law.

The mother-in-law's eyes twinkled. "I believe my son said that his children were not to move around in the nest," she said with a laugh. "I wonder how he is going to stop their doing so."

"Tell them, I suppose," answered young Mrs. Swift, smilingly. "Did he push around at all when he was a baby?"

"He?" replied the older Swift. "He was the most restless child I ever hatched. He will know more about bringing up children after he has raised a brood or two. Don't worry, my dear. It will come out all right." She flew off and the young wife went for twigs also, and thought how happy she ought to be in having such a mother-in-law.

When the lowest nest was built and the four long pure white eggs were laid in it, Mr. and Mrs. Swift were a very proud young couple. The nest was so thin that one could see the eggs through it quite plainly, but it was exceedingly stout and firm. It was not a soft nest, and it had no real lining, although Mrs. Swift had laid in one especially perfect grass blade "to give it style."

That grass blade may be seen to this day by any one who cares to look at the nest as it lies in a cabinet in the house. It was the only nest in the chimney which had anything but twigs in it, and some people wondered at Mrs. Swift's taste. One stout elderly mother Swift said "she supposed it was all right, but that she had never done such a thing and her children had turned out all right." However, young Mrs. Swift smiled in her pretty way and did not talk back.

When they were planning for the four children whom

they expected, Mrs. Swift spoke of how patient they would have to be with them, but Mr. Swift said: "They must be brought up to mind! If I tell a child once to do a thing, that is enough. You will see how I bring them up." Then he ruffled up his feathers, puffed out his throat, and looked very important.

They did most of their visiting in the beautiful night-time, for it is a custom among their people to fly and hunt and visit in the dark, and rest by day. Their busiest time is always just before the sun comes up, and so it happened that the Little Boy who slept in the room below did not often hear the rumbling noise in the chimney as they flew in and out. When they were awakened he slept quietly in his snug little bed, and as he was awakening, and stretching, and getting his dimples ready for the day, the Swifts were going to sleep after a busy night.

When the baby Swifts broke their shells and were seen for the first time by their loving father and mother, Mr. Swift was surprised to find how small they were. Mrs. Swift murmured sweet words to them and worked as hard as her husband to find them food. There were now so many mouths to be fed that they flew by day as well as by night, and often the Little Boy in the room below thought he heard distant thunder when it was only the Swifts coming down the chimney with food for their babies. All sorts of tiny winged creatures were brought them to eat, for Swifts catch all their food as they fly, and that means that they can feed upon only such creatures as also fly.

When they were stretching up to reach the food, Mrs. Swift would say to the children: "Now learn to move carefully, for if you should get over the edge of the nest you will tumble down into that fireplace of which I have told you."

When he was feeding them Mr. Swift would say: "You may open your bills, but not one of you must move beyond that twig. Do you understand?"

Three of them obeyed without asking questions, but the eldest brother was always trying to see just how far he could go without tumbling, and he would talk back to his father.

"You don't care if I put one wing out, do you?" he would ask.

"Not one wing!" his father would answer.

"Why?" the son would ask. "I wouldn't tumble just because I put one wing out."

"It is not minding me," his father would say, "to see how far you can go without tumbling. I did not tell you only to keep from falling out. I told you to keep inside that twig."

Then the son would pout his bill and act very sulky, getting close to the twig which he had been told not to pass. When he thought his father was not looking, he would even wriggle a little beyond it. Mrs. Swift was worried, but what could she do? She noticed that her husband did not talk so much as he used to about making a child mind the very first time he is spoken to.

One night when the Swifts had fed their children faithfully, this son was unusually naughty. It may be that he had eaten more than his share or that he had picked for the biggest insect every time that lunch was brought. It may be, too, that he was naughty simply because he wanted to be. It does not always mean that a child is ill when he is naughty. His father had just told him to be more careful, and he made a face (yes, he did) and flopped aside to show what he could do without falling.

Then he felt a tiny twig on the edge of the nest break beneath him, and he went tumbling, bumping, and scraping down into the fireplace below. He could not fly up, for his wings were not strong enough to carry him up such a narrow space, and his parents could not get him. He heard his brother and sisters crying and his mother saying that she had always expected that to happen.

"Horrid old twig!" he said. "Don't see why it had to break! Should think they might build their nest stronger. I don't care! I was sick of being told not to wriggle, anyway!"

Then he fluttered and sprawled through a crack beside the screen of the grate until he was out in the room. The Little Boy lay asleep in the bed, and that frightened the young Swift. When they tried to scare each other the children had always pretended that a Boy was after them. He crawled behind a picture which leaned against the wall, and stayed there and thought about his dear, dear home up in the chimney.

The Little Boy stirred and awakened and called out: "Mother! Mother! There is somefing making a scratching noise in my room. I fink it is a Bear."

The young Swift sat very still while the Lady came in and hunted for the Bear. She never came near his hiding-place, and laughed at the Little Boy for thinking of Bears. She told him that the only Bears around their town were two-legged ones, and when he asked her what that meant she laughed again.

He peeped out from behind the picture and saw the

Little Boy dress himself. He heard him say: "I can't poss'bly get vese shoes on, but I'll try and try and try." He thought how much pleasanter it was to be a Swift and have all his clothes grow on, and to go barefoot all the year.

He heard the Lady say: "Why, you precious Boy! You did get your shoes on, after all." Then he saw them go off to breakfast, racing to see who would beat.

After they were gone, he fluttered out to the window, and there the Lady found him, and the Little Boy danced around and wanted to touch him, but didn't quite dare. The Lady said: "I think this must have been your Bear," and the Little Boy said: "My teeny-weeny little bitty Bear wiv feavers on." He heard the Little Boy ask, too, why the bird had so many pins sticking out of his tail, and this made him cross. He did not understand what pins were, but he felt that anybody ought to know about tail-quills.

He didn't know much about Boys, for this was the first one he had ever seen, and he wondered what those shiny white things were in his mouth. He had never seen teeth and he could not understand. He wondered how the Boy got along without a bill, and pitied him very much. This Little Boy did not seem so very terrible. He even acted a bit afraid of the Swift.

Next the young Swift felt himself lifted gently in the Lady's hand and laid in a box with soft white stuff in it and two small holes cut in the cover. He was carried from room to room in the house and shown to other people. Once he heard a queer voice say, "Meouw!" and then the Little Boy stamped his foot and said: "Go way, Teddy Silvertip. You can't have my little bird, you hungry Cat."

After this the young Swift was more scared than before, and would have given every feather he had to be safely back in the nest in the chimney. He was hungry, too, and he wanted to see his father and his dear mother. He beat his wings against the sides of the box and cried for his mother. "Oh," he said, "if I were only back in the nest I wouldn't move. I wouldn't move a bit." Then the Cat mewed again and he kept still from fright.

At last he was taken into the open air and placed in the top of a short evergreen, where the Cat could not reach him. Here he clung, weak and lonely and scared, blinking his half-blinded eyes in a light brighter than he had yet seen. All the rest of that day he stayed there, while his father and mother and their other children were sleeping in the home nest. He expected never to see them again, but he did want to tell them how sorry he was.

After the sun had set and the moon was shining, he saw his father darting to and fro above him. "Father!" he cried. "Father, I am so sorry that I moved past the twig. I was very naughty."

His father heard and flew down to tuck a fat and juicy May Beetle into his mouth. "You poor child!" said he. "Eat that and don't try to talk. You will not do such things when you are older. I will get you some more food."

When he returned Mrs. Swift was with him, and they petted and fed the young Swift all night, never scolding him at all, because, as they said, he had been punished quite enough and was sorry. And that was true. His grandmother came also with a bit of food. She told him that they would feed him every night and that he should hide in the branches each day until his feathers were grown.

"In three days more," said she, "you will be ready to fly, and you look more like your father all the time. In three days more," she said, "if nobody eats you up."

You can imagine how anxious the young Swift was during those three days, and how small he tried to be when Silvertip was around. "Surely," he thought, "the sun and moon were never before so slow in marking off the time."

When at last he was ready for flight, Silvertip was under the snowball bush near by. The young Swift sprang into the air. "Good-by, my Cat friend," said he. "You look hungry, but you have lost your best chance at me. You should have been waiting at the grate for me. You might have known that such a foolish young Swift as I would tumble down sooner or later. All that saves some people is not having their foolishness found out!"

THE VERY RUDE
YOUNG ROBINS

W HY this pair of Robins chose to build so near the
Sparrows, nobody knows. It was not at all like Robins
to do so, for they are quite careful how they bring up their
children. One would expect them to think how likely the
little Robins would be to grow up rude and quarrelsome.

However, there their nest was, not the length of a bean-
pole from those of two pairs of Sparrows. When the nestlings
were hatched, they listened all day to what the Sparrows
were saying and looked at what they were doing. They heard
and saw many things which Mr. and Mrs. Robin did not
like. But there was no helping it then, and all that their
parents could do was to try to bring them up to be good
little birds, and do as they had been told, and not as they
had seen naughty children do.

It did make a difference in the behavior of the children,
however, and after they left the nest this showed very plainly.
When they were old enough to go outside the yard in which
they had been hatched, they went to the place next door.
There were many fowls on this place, and several Hens in
coops with young Chickens around them. The father and

mother left the young Robins in safe places while they went to hunt Worms in the newly hoed garden. Two children, a brother and a sister, were half hidden under the drooping branches of a large gooseberry bush.

They had been there for some time, when the sister said, "Just see what lots of good, clean food that Hen and her Chickens have. Don't you wish you had some of it?"

"Um-hum!" answered the brother. "What a pretty yellow it is. I just know it is good!"

Neither of them spoke again for a long time. Indeed, the brother had begun to settle his head down on his shoulders and slide the thin lids over his eyes, when his sister said, "If you were a Sparrow, you'd get some."

"Well, I'm not a Sparrow," he answered, "and so I shall have to go without."

He was almost cross to his dear little sister, but perhaps one could partly excuse him. He saw that there was much more than the Chickens could eat, and that it would lie there spread out on the board until they had spoiled it all by trampling it with muddy feet. Now it was lovely, clean, sweet corn-meal mush. Besides, he was becoming dreadfully hungry. It was fully ten minutes, you know, since he had been fed anything.

The little sister kept still for a while. Her mother had taught her that it does not always pay to talk too much. At last she asked, "Do you suppose those tiny bits of Chickens know the difference between a Sparrow and a Robin?"

Her brother opened his eyes very wide, and stretched his head up so that one could see the black and white feathers under his bill. He was almost full-grown. "I've a good mind to try to fool them," he said. "You see, the Hen can't reach the board where the food is."

"I dare you to!" cried his sister, who really should have been his brother, she was so brave.

"All right," he answered. "Only you come too."

"I will," she said. "But let's wait until Father and Mother are looking the other way."

Twice they started out and came back because their parents were looking. At last they made a dash and were by the board.

"Stand aside!" said the brother, talking as nearly like a Sparrow as he could. "Let us have some of this!"

"Who are you?" asked the Chickens, while the old Hen cluck-cluck-clucked and strutted to and fro in the coop. Every little while she stuck her head out as far as she could reach, and her neck feathers spread around in a funny, fat way against the slats of her coop.

"Go away!" she scolded. "Go right away! That is not your mush! You are not my Chickens! Go right home to your mother! Cr-r-r-r-r!" She said this last, you know, because she was getting so angry that she could say nothing else.

The fowls behind the netting of the poultry-yard all came to see what was going on, and chattered about it in their cackling way. "Send them off!" they cried. "Send them off! The idea of their trying to take food from the Chickens!" The Cocks looked particularly big and fierce. Still, there is not much fun in looking big and fierce behind a wire netting, when the people whom you want to scare are in front of it.

The young Robins were dreadfully frightened, but having feathers all over their face, it did not really show. Neither one was willing to be the first to start away, and they didn't like to speak about it to each other for fear of being overheard. You know, if you can keep other people from finding out that you are scared, you may end by scaring them, and that was exactly what the Robins meant to do.

"Get out of our way!" said they. "Don't brush against us so again! If you were not young, we wouldn't have stood it this time. When you have feathers you may know better."

Then the little Chickens were very badly scared indeed. They backed away as quickly as they could, and crawled in beside their mother. She told them to go back; that the Robins couldn't hurt them, and that she was ashamed to have them act so Chicken-hearted.

"Let us get under your wings!" they said. "Please let us get under your wings!" And they followed, peeping, after her, as she marched to and fro in the narrow coop. Sometimes they got so near her feet that she almost knocked them over, and at last they quite gave up trying to cuddle down under her, and got together in little groups in the back part of the coop.

"Had enough?" asked the brother at last.

"Yes, indeed," answered his sister. "I can't swallow any more now. I'm just making believe because you are not through."

"All right!" said he.

He turned to the Chickens. "Now you may come," he said. "But another time get out of our way more quickly." Then they turned their backs and hopped off. They didn't want to try flying, because that would show how very young they were.

"We did it," exclaimed those two naughty children. "Did

you ever see such little Geese as those Chickens? But oh, what if our parents should find it out?"

"See here," chirped their mother, who could not speak very plainly because she had two large Earthworms hanging in wriggling loops from her bill, "Here is a lovely lunch for you."

"Give it to Brother," said the little sister. "He always wants more than I."

"Oh, no. Give it to Sister," said he. "I don't mean to be selfish."

"You shall both have some," said their mother, tucking a large Worm down each unwilling throat. "Little birds will never be big birds unless they eat plenty of the right kind of food. I will bring you more."

When she was gone they looked at each other. "I just can *not* eat another billful," said the sister.

"And I won't!" said the brother. After a while he added, "Is there any of that mush sticking to my bill?"

"No," said the sister. "Is there any on mine?"

They did not feel at all sure that their mother would have let them eat so much mush if she had been asked. They wondered if it would make them sick. They began to think about the stomach-ache, and felt sure that they had one—that is to say, two—one apiece, you know.

Over in the garden, Mrs. Robin said to her husband, "Do you know what those children have done? It was a very ill-bred, Sparrow-like trick. They scared the little Chickens away, and ate all they could of their mush. I am dreadfully ashamed of them, but I shall pretend I did not see it."

"Make them eat plenty of Worms," suggested Mr. Robin.

"Just what I am going to do," answered his wife. "It won't

really hurt them to overeat for once in their lives, and it will punish them very well."

That was why Mr. and Mrs. Robin worked so especially hard all morning, and made so many trips in under the gooseberry bush. The two young Robins who were there kept insisting that they didn't need any more, and that they really couldn't eat another Worm. After they said this, Mrs. Robin always looked sharply at them and asked, "What have you children been doing? Young birds should always want all the Worms their parents can bring them."

The little Robins were not brave enough to tell what they had done. You know it often takes more courage to confess a fault than it does to scare people. So whenever their mother said this they agreed to eat one more Worm apiece, and choked and gulped it down. It was a dreadful morning for them.

Inside the Chicken-coop the old Hen was trying to settle down again, and the Chickens were talking it over.

"Wasn't it dreadful?" asked one. "I didn't know that Robins were so fierce."

"Mother said that we shouldn't be afraid of them," cried another, "but I guess she'd be afraid her own self if she wasn't in that coop. She'd be 'fraider if she was little, too."

"I'm glad they didn't eat it all," said a third Chicken. "When do you suppose they'll come again?"

"Every day," said another, a Chicken who always expected bad things to happen. "Perhaps they will come two times a day! Maybe they'll even come three!"

But they didn't. They didn't come at all. And they never wanted corn-meal mush again.

THE SYSTEMATIC YELLOW-BILLED CUCKOO

THE people who lived in the big house were much worried about the maple trees which shaded the sidewalk around the place. It was spring now, and they feared another such summer as the last, when the lawn had been covered with fine, healthy, large maple leaves, gnawed off by hungry Caterpillars. One could be sure they were not blown or knocked off, for each stem was neatly eaten through at about the length of a fir needle from the leaf. The lawn did not look well, and the Man who cared for it grumbled and scolded under his breath as he went around raking them up. He could not see that the Caterpillars were of any use in the world. The birds thought differently, but he was a busy Man and not used to thinking of things in that way.

Now spring had come again, and every day the people looked for more leaves on their lawn. They had not found them yet, because the Caterpillars were not old enough to nibble through the stems. Then, one morning while they were eating their breakfast, these people heard a new voice outside. It was not a sweet voice. It sounded somewhat like a thumping on rough boards. It was saying, "Kuk-kuk-kuk!"

Some men who were passing by stopped to look up at the trees, then shook their heads and went on. The Little Boy wanted to leave his breakfast and go out at once to find the new bird, but he had to stay where he was, eat slowly, and fold his napkin before he was allowed to do this. When he went, the Lady and the Gentleman went with him. None of them could see the bird, although they heard his "kuk-kuk-kuk!" in first one tree and then another.

"I am sure that is a Yellow-billed Cuckoo," said the Lady, "and if it is, he has come for the Caterpillars that are spoiling our trees."

"Why, Mother?" asked the Little Boy. "How do you know? You didn't see him."

"If you had your eyes shut, and I spoke to you," she replied, "wouldn't you known whose voice it was?"

The other birds also seemed to know whose voice it was, for they flew around in fright, and scolded and chattered until the visitor had left that row of maples and gone far away. Even then the more timid ones could not settle down to their regular duties. "It has given me such a start," said one Robin, whose nerves were always easily upset, "that I don't believe I can weave another grass-blade into my nest to-day."

"Nonsense!" exclaimed a Blackbird. "Eat something and you will feel all right. There is nothing like eating to make one feel better."

The Robin did as she was told and felt somewhat steadier, yet even then she talked of nothing else that morning. "To think of a Yellow-billed Cuckoo coming here!" she said. "It makes my quills tingle to think of it. My poor babies! My poor babies!"

"Couldn't you stop worrying for a while?" her husband asked. "You know you have not even laid your eggs, so your children are not in danger yet."

Mr. Robin was always gentle with his wife. The other birds didn't see how he could stand it, for she was forever worrying about something.

"No," she replied, "they are not laid yet, but they will be, and you know perfectly well, Mr. Robin, how glad that dreadful Cuckoo would be to suck every one of them. If he were only a Black-billed Cuckoo, it would not be so bad, but I saw his bill quite plainly, and it was yellow. Besides, he said, 'Kuk-kuk-kuk!' instead of 'Kow-kow-kow-kuk-kuk!'"

"We will guard the nest carefully when the eggs are laid," said Mr. Robin. "And now I think I will go across the street to hunt." That also was a wise thing to do, for Mrs. Robin was always more sensible when she was alone.

The birds saw nothing more of the Cuckoo that morning, but in the afternoon he came again. He was a large and very fine-looking bird, with green-gray feathers on the upper part of his body and in the middle of his tail, the outer tail-feathers being black with white spots. His wings were a bright brown, and the under part of his body was grayish-white. His bill was a very long and strong one, and the under half of it was yellow.

He had a habit of sitting very quietly every now and then on some branch to think. At such times he looked handsome but stupid, and really, when he got to thinking so, he was in great danger. It is at just such times that Hawks like to find Cuckoos, and after a Hawk has found one, nobody else ever has a chance. If you remember what sort of food Hawks like, you will understand what this means.

When he was flying, however, he was exceedingly careful, always flitting from tree to tree by the nearest way, and never talking until he was well sheltered again by leafy branches. When he came to a row of maples, he began at one end and went right through, stopping a little while in each to hunt. He was very systematic, and that, you know, means that he always tried to do the same things in the same way. This was why, during all the summer that followed, he came both morning and afternoon at just the same times as on that first day. That is, he did on every day but one.

Mrs. Cuckoo looked exactly like her husband. Indeed, some of their neighbors could hardly tell them apart. She was a very poor housekeeper. Her nest was only a few sticks laid on a bush in the edge of an orchard. She often said that she did not take easily to home life, so many of her great-grandparents having built no nests at all, but laid their eggs in the homes of other birds. Since this was so, people should not have expected too much of Mrs. Cuckoo.

Another thing which made it hard for her, was the way in which she had to lay eggs, hatch eggs, and feed nestlings at the same time all summer. This was not her fault, for of course when an egg was ready it had to be laid, and there were seldom two ready at once. It kept her busy and worried and tired all summer, and one could forgive her if she sometimes grew impatient.

"I can never half do anything after my first egg is hatched," she used to say. "I go to get food for that child, and all the time I am worrying for fear the second egg, which I have just laid, will get cold. Of course one newly hatched nestling cannot keep a large egg like mine warm. Then, when I am having all I can do to care for child and egg, I have to stop to lay another egg."

Mr. Cuckoo was always sleek and respectable-looking. He never seemed in a hurry. He said that haste was ill-mannered. "Always take time," he said, "to do things in the best way. If you are not sure which is the best way, sit down and think about it." He was much annoyed by Mrs. Cuckoo, and often told her how she needed to be systematic. "You have such a hurried way, my dear," said he. "It is really very disagreeable."

She was naturally a sweet-tempered bird, but one day she made up her mind to let her husband see how systematic he could be in her place. At that time she had a young bird and two eggs in the nest, and was very sure that one of the eggs was about to hatch.

When they awakened the next morning, she said sweetly to Mr. Cuckoo, "My dear, please stay with the baby until I get back." Then she flew away without giving him time to ask how long it would be or anything about it. Mr. Cuckoo was much surprised, and sat there thinking, as you know he was likely to do, until the nestling fairly screamed for food.

"Dear me!" said he to himself, "I must do something to keep that child still." So he hunted food and stuffed it down the nestling's wide-open bill. While he was doing so, he remembered the eggs, which he found rather cool. "She will never forgive me if those get cold," he said, so he hopped onto the nest and covered them with his breast. He wished that his wife would return. He thought that when a mother-bird had home cares she should stay by the nest. Just then his child cried for more food.

"Hush!" he exclaimed. "I cannot go now. Don't you see that I am warming these eggs?"

"I don't care! I am hungry," cried she. "You didn't feed me enough."

"Well, I couldn't get you more just then," he said. "Now be patient until your mother comes. That's a good child."

"I can't be patient. I'm hungry," cried the nestling. "I want a Caterpillar."

Mr. Cuckoo could not stand teasing, so he hopped off the nest and picked up the first Caterpillar he found. It was not a good kind, and the little Cuckoo made a bad face and would not swallow it. Mr. Cuckoo rushed away to get a better one. That was eaten, and he was just getting on the eggs again when he heard a faint tapping inside of one. This made him very nervous, for he was not used to caring for newly hatched children. He called several times to Mrs. Cuckoo, but received no answer.

There was more tapping, and the second child stuck his little bill through the shell and broke it. "Ouch!" cried the older one; "that pricks me. Take it away!"

"'Sh!" exclaimed his father, who knew that it would never do to help a young bird out of its shell. The elder child began to cry.

Well! You can just imagine what kind of morning Mr. Cuckoo had. He had to quiet and feed the older child, clear away the broken shell when the second was out, keep the remaining egg warm, get some food for himself, and just hurry and worry until noon. He was about worn out when his wife came back. She looked very trim and happy, and there was no ill-mannered haste in her motions as she flew toward the nest.

"I have had such a pleasant morning," she said. "I met my sister and we went hunting together. I hope you did not mind. I felt quite easy about everything. I knew that you would manage it all beautifully, because you are so systematic." She looked at him with such a sweet smile that he did not say any of the things which he had been planning to say about mother-birds staying at home.

Just then the elder nestling said, "I'm hungry, Mother! I haven't had a Caterpillar in ever so long."

Mrs. Cuckoo answered cheerfully, "All right, I'll get you one," and was about to start off when Mr. Cuckoo spoke up:

"You stay here and look after your newly hatched nestling," said he. "I'll get some food."

Mrs. Cuckoo was delighted to find another egg hatched, and the morning away had been a great rest to her. Only one thing troubled her. "I do wish," she murmured, "that I could have seen Mr. Cuckoo trying to do three or four things at once and be systematic. Now I shall never know how it worked."

But she did know. Her first-hatched child said, "I'm so glad you are back. It made Father cross to hurry." She also knew from another thing: Mr. Cuckoo never again told her to be systematic, or said that it was ill-mannered to hurry.

And that was the one day when Mr. Cuckoo did not make his two regular hunting trips through the maple trees around the big house.

THE HELPFUL TUMBLE-BUGS

In the corner of the barnyard was a pile of manure which was to be put upon the garden and plowed in. This would make the ground better for all the good things growing in it, but now it was waiting behind the high board fence, and many happy insects lived in it. There were big Bugs and little Bugs, fat Bugs and slim Bugs, young Bugs and old Bugs, good Bugs and—well, one does not like to say that there were bad Bugs, but there were certainly some not so good as others.

Among all these, however, there were none who worked harder or thought more of each other than the Tumble-bugs. One couple, especially, were thrifty and devoted. They had been married in June, when each was just one day old. June weddings were the fashion among their people.

Mr. Tumble-bug believed in early marriages. "I have known Tumble-bugs," he said, "who did not marry until they were two days old, but I think that a great mistake. Each becomes so used to having his own way that it is very hard for husband and wife to agree on anything. Now Mrs. Tumble-bug and I always think alike." Then he smiled at Mrs. Tumble-bug and Mrs. Tumble-bug smiled at him.

They were nearly always together and busy. Perhaps it was because they worked together every day that they cared so much for each other. You know that makes a great difference, and if one had worked all the time while the other was playing, they would soon have come to care for other things and people.

One hot summer morning, Mrs. Tumble-bug said to her husband, who was just finishing his breakfast, "I have found the loveliest place you ever saw for burying an egg-ball. Do hurry up! I can hardly wait to begin work."

Mr. Tumble-bug gulped down his last mouthful and answered, "I'm ready now."

"Follow me then," she cried, and led the way over all sorts of little things which littered up the ground of the barnyard. No Horse was there just then, and she felt safe. Mr. Tumble-bug followed close behind her, and a very neat-looking couple they made. Both were flat-backed and all of shining black. "We do not dress so showily as some Bugs," they were in the habit of saying, "but black always looks well." And that was true. Although they spent most of their days working in the earth, they were ever clean and shining, with smiling, shovel-shaped faces.

"There!" said Mrs. Tumble-bug, as she stopped for breath and pointed with her right fore-leg to the ground just ahead of her. "Did you ever see a finer place?" She could point in this way, you know, without falling over, because she had five other legs on which to stand. There are some very pleasant things about having six legs, and the only tumbling she and her husband did was part of their work.

"Excellent!" exclaimed Mr. Tumble-bug. "And the ground

is so soft that it will not tire you very much to dig in it." He did not have to think whether it would tire him, because he never helped in that part of the work. His wife always liked to do that alone.

Then both Tumble-bugs scurried back to the manure heap. "I cannot see why some of our neighbors are so foolish," said she. "There is a Beetle now, laying her eggs right in this pile. She will leave them there, too, and as likely as not some hungry fellow will come along before the sun goes down and eat every one of them. She might much better take a little trouble, put her egg in a mass of food, and roll it away to a safe place for burial. When my children hatch out into soft little Grubs, I intend they shall have a chance to grow up safely and comfortably. Such Beetles do not deserve to have children."

"Well, they won't have many," said her husband. "Perhaps only a pitiful little family of twenty or thirty."

"Now," exclaimed Mrs. Tumble-bug, "We must get to work. Help me roll this ball of manure. I have laid an egg in it while we were talking, so that time was not wasted."

Together they rolled a ball which was bigger than both of them when it started, and grew larger and larger as they got it away from the heap and the dust of the ground stuck to it and crusted it over.

Mrs. Tumble-bug stood on top of the ball, and, creeping far out on it, pulled it forward with her hind feet, while he stood on his head behind it and pushed with his hind legs. Of course if Mrs. Tumble-bug had not been climbing backward all the time, the ball would have rolled right over her. To pull forward with part of your legs and climb backward with all of them at the same time, and that when your head is a good deal lower than your heels, is pretty hard work and takes much planning. Mrs. Tumble-bug had very little breath for talking, but she did not lose her temper. And that shows what an excellent Bug she was. "Harder!" she would call out to Mr. Tumble-bug. "We are coming to a little hill."

Then Mr. Tumble-bug, who, you will remember, had to stand on his head all the time, and really did the hardest part of the work, would brace himself more firmly and push until it seemed as though his legs would break. He could never see just where they were going unless he let go of the ball, and Mrs. Tumble-bug did not believe in turning out for anything.

"What if there is a hill?" she often said. "Can't we go over it?" And over it they always went, although they might much more easily have gone around it. Mrs. Tumble-bug did not want anybody to think her afraid of work, and she knew her husband would have a chance to rest while she was burying the ball. Once in a while, when the ball came down suddenly on the farther side of a twig or chip, it rolled quite on top of her, and Mr. Tumble-bug would be greatly alarmed. Some people thought this served her quite right for insisting that they should go over things instead of around them. Still, one hardly likes to say a thing like that.

If it were much of a hill, she would climb down from the ball and talk with him. Then they would put their shovel-shaped heads together under the back side of the ball, and, pushing at the same time, send it over. "Two heads are better than one," they would say, "and this needs a great deal of head-work."

At last the ball had reached the spot where they intended to have it buried. Both were hot and tired. "Many legs make light work," said Mrs. Tumble-bug, as she carefully cleaned hers before eating dinner, "and if there is anything I enjoy, it is finishing a good job like this!"

Mr. Tumble-bug sighed heavily and said he thought he would go for a walk with some of his friends that afternoon. "All work and no play would make me a dull Bug," said he. Then he called out "Good-by" to his wife, and told her not to work too hard.

Mrs. Tumble-bug looked after him lovingly. "Now, isn't he good?" she said to herself. "There are not many Bugs who will help their wives at all, and most of them never look at an egg, much less see to getting it well placed." And that is true, for the Tumble-bugs are the model Bug fathers.

Now, indeed, Mrs. Tumble-bug was at her best. She hurried down her dinner, taking mouthfuls which were much too large for good manners, and began plowing the earth around the ball as it lay there. She plowed so deep that sometimes she was almost buried in the loose earth. At last she came up, took a good look around, knocked some grains of dust off her shining back, then dived in again upside down, and pulled the ball in after her by holding it tightly with her middle legs. All the time she was kicking the earth away with her two hind legs and her two front ones, which were stout diggers, so that little by little she sank deeper into the ground.

She made a much larger hole for the ball than it really needed. "I might just as well, while I am about it," she said. "And I should so dislike to have any one think me afraid of work."

At last she finished and crawled away, covering the place neatly over, so that nobody could see where she went in or out. "There!" she said. "Now I am ready to play."

A stray Chicken came along and she hurried under a chip to be safe. The Chicken was lost and calling to his mother. "Mother!" he cried. "Mother Hen, I want to get home and go to sleep under your wings."

"Dear me!" exclaimed Mrs. Tumble-bug. "Is it time for Chickens to go to sleep?" She looked through a crack in the fence and across the lawn to the big house. The shadows lay long upon the short grass. "It certainly is," she said. "And here I have spent all day burying that egg properly. I think it very strange that I cannot get more time for rest and play." So she had to eat her supper and go straight to bed to get rested for the next day's work.

Mrs. Tumble-bug did not understand then, and perhaps never will learn, that if she would stop doing things in the hardest way and begin doing them in the easiest way, she might get a great deal of work done in a day and still have time to rest. If one were to tell her so, she might think that meant laziness, but it would not, you know. It is always worth while to make one's head save one's feet, and when a single head could save six feet it would certainly be worth while. Still, although Mrs. Tumble-bug never dreamed of such a thing, she probably enjoyed work about as much as her neighbors enjoyed play.

SILVERTIP LEARNS A LESSON

You may remember what a funny time Silvertip had with the first Mouse he caught; how he carried it so long in his mouth before daring to lay it down, and how frightened he was each time that it wriggled. That was because he was just beginning to hunt. Cats have to learn by doing things over and over, just like other people. He used to hear the Little Boy sing.

If at first you do not try   Try, try again.

After a while he heard him sing.

If at first you don't succeed   Try, try again.

He did not understand just what this meant, but he soon knew that Little Boys have to learn things quite as Cats do. He watched him afterward learning to turn summersaults, and saw him do just that and nothing else for nearly a whole afternoon.

It was in some such way that Silvertip came to be a good hunter. He used to spend whole hours under the low branches of some evergreen, crouching and springing at every passing bird. In summer he crawled through the wheat-field back of the house, looking for Mice. If he found nothing better, he caught Moles, although he never ate them. He thought that Moles were probably made for Cats to practice on, and that good little Cats, who did the best they could on Moles, would find Mice to catch after a while—if they were patient.

When he could not find anything alive to hunt, he practiced on the dead leaves which were blown over the lawn, or chased empty spools across the kitchen floor. In the spring, when the Gentleman went out before breakfast to work in his garden, Silvertip played with the onion sets, chasing them down the narrow trench in which they had been placed, until the Gentleman had to carry him off and shut him up.

This is how he became so fine a hunter, and it is perhaps not strange that after a while he grew conceited. You know what it means to be conceited. Well, Silvertip was so. He thought himself really the cleverest Cat that had ever lived, a Cat who could catch anything he tried to. He bragged to the other Cats who came around, and when he was alone he purred to himself about the fine things he could do. Now people who think themselves clever are not always conceited, for sometimes they are as clever as they think. But when a person is always thinking and talking about what he can do, you watch him to see if he does as well as he thinks. If not, then he is conceited.

Silvertip even used to climb nearly to the top of the tall maple-trees after Blackbirds, and crouch there, switching his tail, yet he never caught any. When the other Cats asked him about this, he would smile, and say that he decided not to eat any more just then, or that he had found that Blackbirds disagreed with him. Undoubtedly these excuses were both true, still they did not keep him from trying again and again.

The only Blackbird he ever caught was a young one who had disobeyed her mother and flopped away from the tangle of rosebushes where she had been told to stay. She was dreadfully punished for it—but then it was very wrong for her not to mind her mother. If she had stayed where she was, the thorns would have kept Cats away.

Silvertip had been in the big house nearly a year, when Mr. Chipmunk came to live in the yard. He chose to burrow under the open shed which ran along by the back fence, and under which wood was piled to dry before it was split and carried into the wood-house. He was the first Chipmunk who had ever lived on the place, and all his new neighbors were much interested in him.

"Shall you bring your family here?" Mr. Robin asked him, as he watched his own children caring for themselves. Mr. Robin had worked hard all summer, and now he was enjoying a little visiting time before starting south.

"My family?" answered Mr. Chipmunk, with a chuckling laugh. "No, indeed! One is company and two is crowd with Chipmunks. Of course mothers have to live with their children for a time, but fathers always have holes to themselves."

Mr. Robin did not think that right, yet he kept still. He knew that it is not always wise or polite to say all that one thinks. He thought it was not fair to make the mothers have all the care of the children. There is great difference in animals about this.

Mr. Chipmunk began at once to dig his burrow. He had not seen Silvertip yet, and did not know that there was a Cat around. He began just in front of the woodpile, and when he had enough earth loosened to fill his cheek-pockets, he brought it out and emptied it by the doorway of his burrow. Quite a pile was there already when Silvertip came walking past.

"Meouw!" said he. "What sort of creature is at work here?"

Mr. Chipmunk heard his voice, and lay still in his burrow. If Silvertip had not spoken just then, this story might end very differently. In fact, it would probably be ended already. "A Cat!" said he. "Well, it is always something, and it might as well be a Cat as a Dog. He won't be so likely to dig me out, anyway."

After a long time he turned around, and went quietly toward the door-way of the burrow, just far enough to see who was there. What he saw was a white face with tiger spots and a pink nose. Long white whiskers stuck out on either side, and the nose was twitching. Silvertip was trying to get a good smell of the new-comer.

Mr. Chipmunk did not move, and being brown and in the darkness of the hole, Silvertip, who stood in the sunshine, could not see him. For a long time neither moved. Then Silvertip walked slowly away. He was not very hungry that morning. Mr. Chipmunk always believed in keeping still as long as possible. "If the other fellow is the larger," said he, "always wait to see what he is going to do. Then you can decide better what you should do."

After this Silvertip came often to the burrow. He learned the Chipmunk by smell long before he saw him. When at last he did see him, Mr. Chipmunk was perched on a low stick of wood, with his small fore paws clasped on his breast and his beautiful fur glistening in the sunshine. He was facing Silvertip, so the Cat did not see the five dark stripes on his back till later.

Silvertip crouched and tried his muscles by shaking himself a little. He did not say that it was a pleasant day, or that he was glad to become acquainted with Mr. Chipmunk. He did not even say, "I see you are making a new home!" He was sure this was the little creature whom he had been smelling for several days, and he saw no use in saying anything. He meant to eat Mr. Chipmunk, and Mr. Chipmunk understood it. There was really nothing to be said. Mr. Chipmunk might object to being eaten. People usually did object to it, but Silvertip saw no sense in talking it over. He would rather have no conversation whatever at meals than to speak of disagreeable things or to quarrel.

Mr. Chipmunk did not care to talk, either. He believed in thinking before you speak, and he had a great deal of thinking to do just then. A team stopped by the gate of the driveway. Mr. Chipmunk dared not look to see what was coming. Silvertip did not look until the Milkman was near him carrying the milk bottles. Then he gave one quick upward glance. When he looked back, the stick of wood was there, but Mr. Chipmunk was gone.

Silvertip was not at all happy, and he felt still worse when Mr. Chipmunk stuck his saucy little face out of the burrow and called, "Chip-r-r-r! Milk is better for Cats anyway, you know!" Mr. Chipmunk did not have to stop to think when he was in his hole.

That was the beginning of the acquaintance, and a very merry one it was for Mr. Chipmunk. "I have to be hunted anyway," he said, "so I might as well have some fun out of it."

Whenever he saw Silvertip having an especially comfortable nap, he would run near and give his chirping, chuckling laugh. Then he would run away. Sometimes he would stand as still as a stone, with his tiny fore paws clasped on his breast. Silvertip would creep and crawl up close to him, and he would act too scared to move. Then, just as Silvertip was ready to spring, he would cry out, "Chip-r-r-r!" and tumble heels over head into his burrow.

Sometimes, too, Silvertip would be walking along as happily as possible, not even thinking of Chipmunks, when a mischievous little face would peep out from the woodpile just beside him. Mr. Chipmunk would say "Good-morning!" then draw back and disappear, only to peep out again and again from new places as the Cat came along. You know nothing can catch a Chipmunk when he is in a woodpile. The worst of it was that there always seemed to be so many other people around to see how poor Silvertip was teased. You would never have thought that Silvertip was hunting Mr. Chipmunk. It always seemed to be Mr. Chipmunk who was hunting Silvertip.

At last Mr. Chipmunk had his burrow all done. He had made an opening at the second end and closed the one at the first, so nobody could tell from the pile of earth what had been happening. He said he had crawled into the hole and pulled it in after him. The last opening, which was now to be his only door, was under the woodpile. No rain could fall into it and no Dog could dig at it. Mr. Chipmunk was very happy.

He made friends with the Lady, too. She seemed to be perfectly harmless, and she brought him a great deal of

MR. CHIPMUNK ON THE WOODPILE.

corn and many peanuts. Sometimes he found butternuts tucked around in the woodpile, which could not possibly have fallen from any tree. He decided that he might come to some sort of agreement with Silvertip. He got ready for it by being more annoying than ever. When Silvertip's tail was switching and his nose twitching with anger, Mr. Chipmunk peeped out from a hollow stick in the pile and called to him.

"Silvertip!" cried he, "O Silvertip! I want to talk with you. How would you like to be eaten up?"

There was no answer, except a murmuring under his breath that he "guessed there wasn't much danger."

"Enjoy the acquaintance, do you, Silvertip?" asked Mr. Chipmunk. "Find me a pleasant talker? Ever tell anybody that you were going to eat me?"

Now Silvertip had told some of his friends exactly that, but this was before he knew so much about Chipmunks. He growled something under his breath about "Quit your teasing."

"I will if you will quit trying to catch me," answered Mr. Chipmunk. "Tell your friends that you changed your mind. Tell them that I am not to your taste. Tell them anything you wish, but let me alone and I will let you alone."

"All right," said Silvertip. "Now don't you ever speak to me again."

"Never!" answered Mr. Chipmunk. "Walnuts couldn't hire me to!" And after that there was peace around the woodpile.

THE ROBINS' DOUBLE BROOD

THE Robins who nested on the west-side second-story window-ledge had four as good children as you would care to see. They were healthy nestlings, brought up to mind and to eat what was given to them without fussing. If, for any reason there came a time when they had to go without for a while, they were good-natured then also. Their parents had raised other broods the year before, and had learned that it is not really kind to children to spoil them.

"You must never forget," Mrs. Robin used to say, "that your father *is* your father and your mother *is* your mother. If it were not for us, you would not be here at all, and if it were not for us you would have nothing to eat now that you are here. Little birds should be very thoughtful of their parents."

When it was bedtime, and the young Robins wanted to play instead of going to sleep, their father would often leave the high branch where he was singing his evening song and come over to talk to them. When he did this he did not scold, but he looked so grave that each child listened to every word. "Your mother," he would say, "has been busy all day, hunting Worms for you and flying up to the nest with them. Now she is tired, and would enjoy perching on a branch and sleeping alone, but because that would leave you cold and lonely she is willing to sleep in the nest and cover you with her soft feathers. Do you think it is fair for you to keep her awake?"

Then all the little Robins would hang their heads and murmur, "No, Father."

"What are you going to do about it?" would be the next question. And then the little Robins never failed to raise their heads and answer, "We will be good and not say a word."

Mrs. Robin often said that there would be more happy mothers in the world if their children took as good care of them as her nestlings took of her. "They have to be reminded," she said, "because they are so young, but when they have been told the right thing to do, they always do it." The Catbird, however, who was a very shrewd fellow, said he thought it was not so much what their father said to them that made them good, as what they saw him do. He was always kind to Mrs. Robin himself, you know, and spoke gently, and left the biggest Worms for her to eat, so his children felt sure that this was the right way.

Mrs. Robin, too, was always polite to her husband. She spoke pleasantly of him to the children, and if he had any faults she did not talk about them. The little Robins were certain that they had the finest father in the world, and meant to be exactly like him when they grew up. That is, the sons did. The daughters meant to be like their mother.

When the little Robins' tail-feathers were about as long as fir needles, they were surprised to find a beautiful blue egg in the nest beside them. "Is it for us to play with?" they asked their mother. "Did we come out of eggs like that? Why is this here?"

Then their wise and gentle mother stood on the ledge beside the nest and talked to them. She was a busy bird, you know, but she always said that it took no longer to answer children's questions than it did to tell them over and over again to keep still.

"Each of you came out of just such an egg as that," she said. "This one is here because I had it ready to lay, and there was no other good place to put it. You may play with it very carefully, and be sure not to push it out of the nest, for then it would fall on the porch roof and break. You may take turns lying next to it, and before long I will lay another, so you can all be next to an egg at the same time."

"What are you going to do with them?" asked the Oldest Nestling. "What will become of them when we are old enough to leave the nest?"

"That is the loveliest part of it," answered their mother. "I shall hatch these eggs, too, and then you can have baby brothers and sisters, perhaps both."

"But who will take care of us?" asked the Youngest Nestling, and she looked as though she wanted to cry when she spoke.

"Don't you worry, little Robin," said her mother cheerfully. "There are always enough people to do the things which have to be done, if they will only keep sweet and not make a fuss. We will all help each other and everything will come out beautifully. This is the first time I ever laid the eggs for the second brood before the first brood was out of the nest, but we shall manage. Besides," she added, "I believe you are the first little Robins I ever knew who had a chance to help hatch eggs before being grown up. Won't that be fine?"

Mrs. Robin looked so bright and happy as she spoke that her children were sure it was going to be great fun, and one and all chirped back, "Oh, let's! We'll hatch them just as hard as we can."

Mrs. Robin fixed them with the new egg in the middle of the nest, and went off to help their father find dinner for them. After they had been fed with about fifteen Worms, she laid the second egg. "That will be all for this brood," she said, "and perhaps it is just as well. Too many eggs would crowd the nest."

Then she told them what wonderful things eggs are; how what is going to be the young bird is at first only a tiny, soft, stringy thing, floating around inside the shell, with a ball of yellow food-stuff in the middle of the shell and clear white stuff all around it. She told them, too, how this little thing which is to be a bird floats on top of the other stuff, and so is always next to the mother's breast as she sits over it on the nest. "It is the being warm for a long time and all the time that changes it into a bird strong enough to break the shell. You will remember that, won't you," said she, "and keep the top side of the eggs warm when I am not here?"

All the little birds were sure that they could, and very proud to think that she would trust them so. Perhaps if she had said, "Now, don't you let me catch you leaving those eggs uncovered!" they might have murmured to each other, "What do we care about her old eggs? Let them get cold!" It is a great pity, you know, when people in families get to talking in that way. And the worst of it is that every time one person speaks so, another is almost sure to answer in the same way.

Now the Robin family were all caretakers, and when Mrs. Robin flew up with choice Worms for her children, she gave them loving glances, and said, "You are such helpers! I don't know how I could get along without you."

Mr. Robin, too, remarked every now and then that it made him happy to see how thoughtful they were of their mother. After he had said these things, the children always stretched themselves, so that they might look as big as they felt.

With four growing children besides the two eggs in the nest, it soon became very much crowded. Mr. and Mrs. Robin talked it over while hunting in the garden, where the Hired Man was spading. After they had fed the children whole billfuls of Worms, which they had found wriggling there on top of the ground, Mr. Robin said: "Now, if you will keep very still and not interrupt, I will tell you some good news."

When all was quiet, he said: "I shall take you out into the great world to-morrow. I shall teach you to fly, to perch on branches, and to hunt for yourselves."

"Oh goody!" cried all the little Robins together. Then they remembered how stubby their wings and tails still were, and wondered how they could ever get to the ground. "Won't we tumble some?" they asked doubtfully.

"You may tumble some," answered their father, "but isn't it worth a tumble to get out into the world? Mother will stay up here and finish hatching the eggs while I am with you, and we will stay near enough for her to see how fast you learn."

You can imagine how excited the young Robins were then. They talked so much that day that not one of them took a nap, and if their mother had not insisted upon it, they would not have quieted down at sunset.

Early the next morning their parents helped them to the ground. First they tumbled, fluttered, and sprawled to the porch roof below the nest. Then when they had rested, they tumbled, fluttered, and sprawled to the tops of the sweetbriar bushes underneath. There they clung until after breakfast, while their father hunted for them and their mother sat on the eggs above. If they had not been taught to mind, it would have been much harder. As it was, when their parents said, "Flutter your wings! Get ready! Fly!" they did the very best they could at once. And that is exactly the way children must do if they wish to grow strong and help themselves.

There never were such plump, cheerful, and obedient little Robins as these. Their father had them stay in the lower branches of the fir tree, within sight of the nest, and the mother watched them while he was hunting, and called down comforting things to them. When they had tumbles in trying to fly, she would say: "Never mind! Pick yourselves up! Robins must tumble before they can fly. After awhile, when I have finished hatching these eggs, you can come right up to this window ledge and see the babies."

Then the little Robins would try harder than ever, for they were already proud of the babies to be hatched, since they had helped keep the eggs warm.

Sometimes Silvertip would stroll around the corner of the house, and Mrs. Robin would be so scared that she could hardly scream "Cat!" Yet she always managed to do it in some way, and all the other Robins would help her. Then the Lady, who was almost always writing or sewing at the sitting-room window, within sight of the nest, would drop her work and run out the nearest door, pick up Silvertip, and carry him inside. There he would stand, with his nose pressed against the screen and his tail switching angrily.

The Lady seemed to understand Robins. When they only cried "Trouble!" she did not move, knowing it was something she could not help, but when they cried, "Cat! Cat!" she always hurried out. Sometimes, though, it was the Gentleman who came, and sometimes the Little Boy. Mrs. Robin often said that she was sure she could never raise children so well in any other place as here, in spite of Silvertip's being around.

Every day the young Robins were larger and stronger, and their tail-feathers were better grown. When at last the joyful time came for the two babies to chip the shell, every one of the four children managed to get up to the window ledge to see them. It was a hard trip, and they had to try and try again, and rest between times. They were not all there at once, but oh, it was a happy, happy time!

The mother told the babies how their big brothers and sisters had helped hatch them, and the father told the mother how beautifully she had managed everything. Then the mother told him how faithfully he had worked, and they both told the older children how proud they were of them. Everybody said lovely things to everybody else, and the best part of it was that all these lovely things were true.

The babies were too little to talk much, but they stretched their necks up lovingly and sleepily to all the family, and acted as though they really understood how many people had been loving and working for them, even before they were hatched.

THE SPARROWS
INSIDE THE EAVES

O NE does not like to say such things, but the English
Sparrows were very disagreeable people. And they are
very disagreeable people. Also, they always have been, and
probably always will be, very disagreeable people. They were
the first birds to make trouble among neighbors anywhere
around the big house. If it had not been that the Gentleman who lived there was so very tender-hearted, their nests
would probably have been poked down with poles long
before the eggs could have been laid in them. When Boys
came around with little rifles and ugly looking bags slung
over their shoulders, they were always ordered away and told
that the Gentleman would have no shooting near his house.

It is not strange then that the woodbine was full of
Sparrows' nests, and that many of the evergreens also bore
them in their top branches. One had even been tucked
in behind a conductor pipe, and their owners hunted and
argued and fussed all over the place. There was just one
way in which the English Sparrows were not cared for like
other birds around the big house. Silvertip was allowed to
eat all that he could catch. And you may be very sure that

no Robin ever called "Cat!" when he was ready to spring upon a Sparrow.

"It may be wrong," said one Robin mother, "but I cannot do it. I remember too well how they have robbed my nests and quarrelled with my friends. I say that they must care for their own children. And if they do not—well, so much the better for Silvertip!"

You see that the birds were not angry at Silvertip for trying to eat them. It was all to be expected, as they knew very well. It was not pleasant, but it had to be, just as Worms and Flies had to expect to be eaten, unless they were clever enough to keep out of the way of birds. Only the quickest and strongest could live, so of course all the young ones tried hard to become quick and strong.

When Miss Sparrow, from the nest behind the conductor pipe, was old enough to marry, she had many lovers, and that was quite natural. She was a plump and trim-looking bird, and pretty, too, if one came close enough to her. Her feathers were gray and brown, with a little white and black in places. Her bill was black, and her feet were brown. She was very careful to keep clean, and although she had to hunt food in the mud of the street, she bathed often in fine dust and kept her wings and tail well up. Her lovers were dressed in the same colors, but with more decided markings.

Her parents were very clever to think of building where they did; and because they had such a large nest and so near the eaves of the house, they were much looked up to by the other Sparrows. They were very proud of their home, and especially on days when the water running down the pipe made a sweet guggle-guggle-guggling sound. Sparrows like noise, you know, and this always amused the children and kept them quiet on rainy days.

All the young Sparrows who were not already in love, and a few who were, began to court Miss Sparrow as soon as it was known that she cared to marry. This was partly on her own account, and partly because of her distinguished family.

Some birds would have waited for their suitors to speak first about marriage. Miss Sparrow did not. The Sparrows are not very well bred. "Of course I am going to marry," she said. "I am only waiting to make up my mind whom I will choose."

They flocked around her as she fed in the dust of the road, all talking at once in their harsh voices. When a team passed by, and that was not often, they flew or hopped aside at the last minute. When they settled down again there was always a squabble to see who should be next to Miss Sparrow. Her lovers fought with each other over choice seeds, but they let Miss Sparrow have everything she wished. She always seemed very cross when her lovers were around (as well as most of the time when they were not), and often scolded and pecked at them. Sometimes one who was not brave, and would not stand pain, flew away and began courting somebody else.

After a while she had driven away so many that only two were left. She flew at these, striking first one and then the other, until, brave as they were, one went away. Then she turned to the suitor who was left with a sweet smile. "I will marry you," she said.

His wings were lame from her fighting him, his head smarted where she had picked at it, and two or three small feathers were missing from his breast. Miss Sparrow was certainly a strong bird, and he knew that anybody who wanted her would have to stand just what he had stood. He would have preferred to court as the Goldfinches and Wrens do, by singing to their sweethearts, but that could not be. In the first place, he could not sing, and in the second place she would not have taken him until she had beaten him anyway. It would have been more fun for him to fight some of the other birds and let the winner have her, yet that could not be done either. If he wanted to marry, he had to marry an English Sparrow, and if he wanted to marry an English Sparrow he had to go about it in her way. It would have been just the same if he had courted her sister or her cousin.

The truth is that, although the Sparrow husbands swagger and brag a great deal and act as though they owned everything in sight, there is not one whose wife does not order him around. Miss Sparrow would not have taken him if she had not made sure that she could whip him.

"What do I need of a husband," she said, "unless he will mind me? And when I feel crosser than usual I want somebody always near and at home, where I can treat him as I choose. That is what I care for in a home."

"Now," she said, "if you are to be my husband, I will show you where we are to build."

Mr. Sparrow flew meekly along after her. You would be meek with lame wings, a sore head, and three feathers off from your breast. She led the way to the front west porch, where the syringa shoots made a little hedge around it and a tall fir tree made good perching places beside it.

"Where are we going to build?" asked Mr. Sparrow. He saw plenty of good window ledges and places which would do for Robins and Phœbes and other birds who plaster their nests. Yet he did not see a single corner or big crack where a Sparrow's nest could be made to hold together.

"I will show you," answered Mrs. Sparrow. She perched on the top of a porch column and looked up at a small round hole nearly over her head. It was the place where a conductor pipe had once run through the cornice. Now the pipe had been taken away and the opening was left. She gave an upward spring and flutter and went straight up through the hole. "Come up!" she cried in the most good-natured way. "Come up! This is the best place I ever saw. Our nest will be all hidden, and no large bird or Squirrel can possibly get in. The rain can never fall on it, and on cold days we shall be warm and snug."

She did not ask him what he thought of it, and he did not expect her to. So he just said, "It is a most unusual place."

"That is what I think," she replied. "Very unusual, and I would not build in the woodbine like some Sparrows. No, indeed! One who has been brought up in style beside a water-pipe, as I was, could never come down to woodbine. It should not be expected."

"I'm sure it was not, my dear," said her husband.

"Very well," said she. "Since you like this place so much, we may as well call it settled and keep still about it until we are ready to build."

Mr. Sparrow had not said that he liked it, yet he knew better than to tell her so. If he did, she might leave him even now for one of her other lovers. He really dreaded getting out through that hole, and let her go while he watched her. She went head first, clinging to the rough edges of the hole with both feet, let go with one, hung and twisted around until she was headed right, then dropped and flew away. Mr. Sparrow did the same, but he did not like it.

After a while they began nest-building, and all the straws, sticks, and feathers had to be dragged up through the little round doorway to the nest. Mrs. Sparrow did most of the arranging, while her husband flew in and out more than a hundred times a day. She was a worker. Any bird will tell you that. Still, you know, there are different ways of working. Some of the people who do the most work make the least fuss. Mrs. Sparrow was not one of these. When she did a thing, she wanted everybody to know it, and since her building-place was hidden she talked all the more to Mr. Sparrow.

"I am going to have a large nest," she said. "So bring plenty of stuff. Bring good things, too," she added. "You have brought two straws already that were really dirty, and this last stick isn't fit to use. I will push it back into a corner."

Mr. Sparrow would have liked to tell her what hard work his was, and ask her to use things he brought, even if they were not quite what she wanted. He was too wise for this, however, so he flew out and pitched into another Sparrow who was getting straws for his wife. He tried to steal his straw, and they fought back and forth until their wives came to see what was the matter and began fighting also. When they stopped at last, the straw had been carried away by a Robin, so neither had it. But they had had a lovely, loud, rough fight, and Sparrows like that even better than straw, so they all felt good-natured again.

Twice Mrs. Sparrow decided to move her nest a little this way or a little that, and such a litter as she made when doing it! Some of the best sticks fell down through the doorway, and the Lady swept them off the porch. Then Mrs. Sparrow scolded her. She was not afraid of a Lady. "She might have left them there," she said. "I would have had my husband pick them up soon. Yesterday she had the Maid put some of her own horrid chairs and tables out here while they were cleaning, and I never touched them."

Mr. Sparrow flew up with a fine Turkey feather. "It came from the Lady's duster," he said. "I think it will give quite an air to your nest."

"Excellent!" cried his wife. "Just wait until I get ready for it." He clung patiently by one foot to the doorway. When that was tired he changed to the other. When that was tired he perched on the top of the column. He was very hungry, and he saw some grain dropped from a passing wagon.

"Hurry up, my dear!" he called. "It is past my dinner-time already."

"Wait until supper then," cried his wife. "As if I hadn't enough to do without thinking about your dinner! Don't let go of it or it will be blown away."

Then Mr. Sparrow lost his temper. He stuck that feather into a crack near by, and flew softly away to eat some grain. He thought he might be back in time to carry in the feather and his wife never know where he had been. Unfortunately, he got to talking and did not hear his wife call him.

"Mr. Sparrow!" said she. "*Mr. Sparrow!* I am ready for that feather."

When he did not answer, she put her head out of the

doorway. There was the Turkey feather stuck into a crack, and in the road beyond was her husband eating happily with several of his friends. She looked very angry and opened her bill to speak. Then she changed her mind and flew quietly off the other way. She went straight to the Horse-block, where another old suitor was, the one who had come so near winning her. "Mr. Sparrow has disobeyed me," she said, "and is actually eating his dinner when he should be waiting by the nest to help me. I believe that I ought to have married you, but better late than never. Come now."

This was how it happened that when Mr. Sparrow's stomach was quite full, and he suddenly remembered his work, he flew back and found the Turkey feather gone. In the eaves overhead he heard Mrs. Sparrow telling somebody else what to do. He tried to force his way up there. Every time he was shoved back, and not very gently either.

"You might better look for another home," said Mrs. Sparrow's voice. "I have found another husband, one who will help me as I wish. Good-by."

That was the ending of Mr. Sparrow's first marriage. It was a very sad affair, and the birds talked of nothing else for a long time afterward. Some said that it served him exactly right, because he married to get into a fine family, when there were dozens of Sparrow daughters much prettier and nicer than the one he chose. There may have been something in this, for certainly if Mrs. Sparrow had not been so sure of finding another to take his place, she would not have turned him out in the way she did. It is said, however, that her second husband had a hard life of it.

A RAINY DAY ON THE LAWN

W HEN the sun rose, that morning late in April, he tried and tried to look at the big house and see what was happening. All he could see was a thick gray cloud veil stretched between him and the earth, and, shine as hard as he might, not a single sunbeam went through that veil.

When the Blackbirds awakened, they found a drizzling rain falling, and hurried on their waterproofs to get ready for a wet time. Blackbirds are always handsome, yet they never look better than when it rains. They coat their feathers with oil from the pockets under their tails, as indeed all birds do, and then they fly to the high branches of some tall and swaying tree and talk and talk and talk and talk. They do not get into little groups and face each other, but scatter themselves around and face the wind. This is most sensible, for if one of them were to turn his back to the wind, it would rumple up his feathers and give the raindrops a chance to get down to his skin. When they speak, or at least when they have anything really important to say, they ruffle their own feathers and stand on tip-toe, but they ruffle them carefully and face the wind all the time.

When the Robins opened their round eyes, they chirped

cheerfully to each other and put on their waterproofs. "Good weather for us," they said. "It will make fine mud for plastering our new nests, and it will bring out the Worms."

The English Sparrows, Goldfinches, and other seed-eaters were not made happy by the rain. With them it was only something to be borne patiently and without complaining. The Hummingbirds found fewer fresh blossoms open on cloudy days, and so had to fly farther and work harder for their food. The Pewees and other fly-catchers oiled their feathers and kept steadily at work.

The birds had not awakened so early as usual, because it was darker. They had hardly got well started on their breakfast before a sleepy little face appeared at the window of the big house and a sleepy little voice called out: "O Mother, it is raining! I didn't want it to rain."

"Foolish! Foolish! Foolish!" chirped the Robins on the lawn. "Boys would know better than to say such things if they were birds."

"Boys are a bother, anyway," said an English Sparrow, as he spattered in the edge of a puddle. "I wish they had never been hatched."

"Ker-eeeee!" said a Blackbird above his head. "I suppose they may be of some use in the world. I notice that the Gentleman and the Lady seem to think a great deal of this one, and they are a very good sort of people."

"I'd like them better if they didn't keep a Cat," said his brother. "Their Cat is the greatest climber I ever saw. He came almost to the top of this maple after me yesterday, and I have seen him go clear to the eaves of the big house on the woodbine."

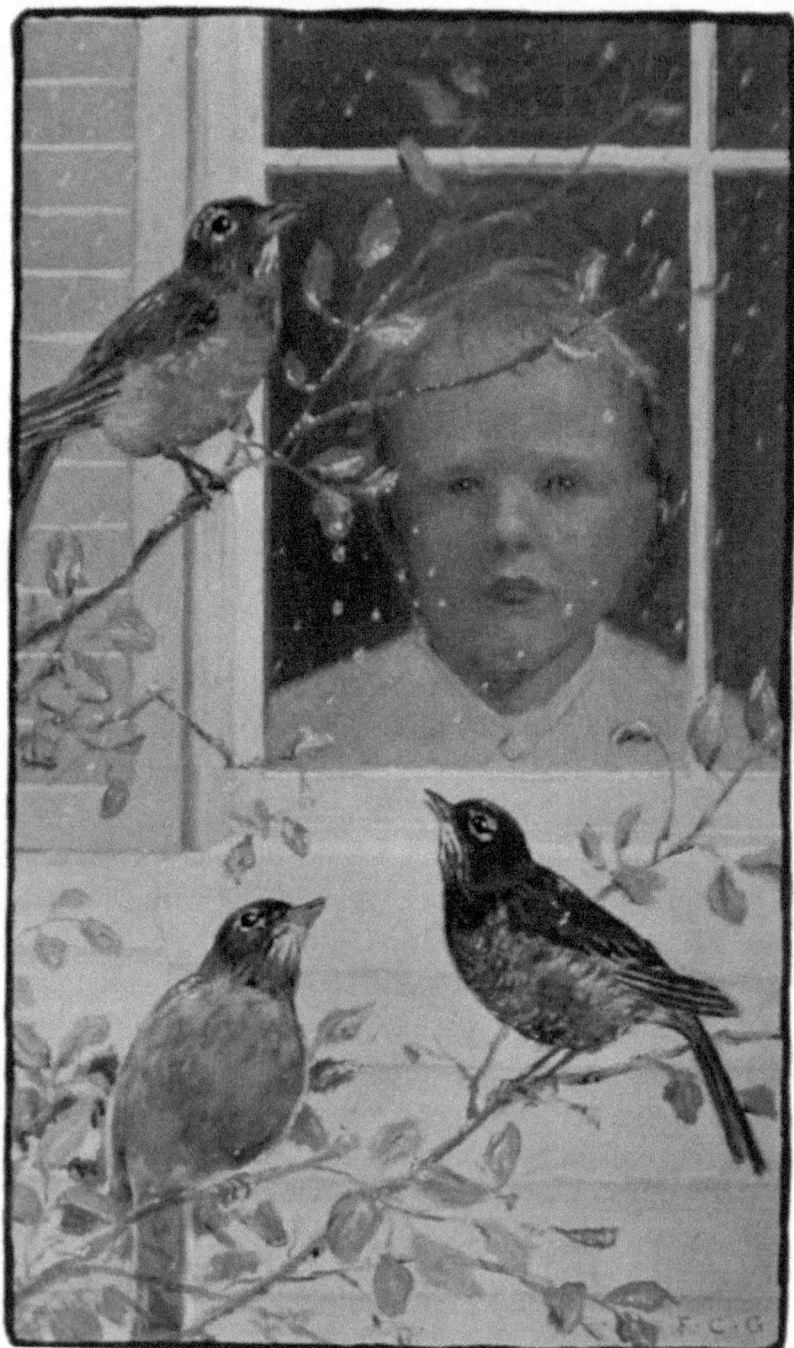

"O MOTHER, IT IS RAINING!"

"That is because the Sparrows live there," said Mr. Wren. "He went to see their children. Silvertip says that he is very fond of children—they are so much more tender than their parents." Mr. Wren could laugh about this because his own children were always safely housed. Besides, you know, he had reason to dislike Sparrows.

"I would not stay here," said a Sparrow who had just come up, "if the people here were not of the right sort. They have mountain ash trees and sweetbrier bushes where birds find good feeding. And in the winter that Boy throws out bread crumbs and wheat for us."

"Humph!" said the Oldest Blackbird. "There is no need of talking so much about it. You can always tell what sort of people live in a place by seeing if they have a bird-house. If they have, and it is a sensible one, where a bird could live comfortably, they are all right."

After that the birds worked more and talked less, for the Oldest Blackbird, while he was often grumpy and sometimes cross, was really a very sensible bird, and what he had said was true. The Robins went here and there over the lawn in quick, short runs, pausing once in a while with their heads bent forward and then pulling up choice Worms to eat. Some of their mouthfuls were half as long as they, but that was not rude in Robins. What they insist on in bringing up their children is that mouthfuls should not be too broad, and that they should not stop swallowing until all the Worm is out of sight.

The Blackbirds hunted in a more dignified way. They never ran after food, or indeed after anything else. "If walking is not fast enough," the Blackbird mothers say, "then fly, but do not run." They walked in parties over the lawn and waggled their heads at each step. When they found Grubs they did not appear greedy, yet never a Grub escaped.

"There are two ways of hurrying," they often said. "One is the jerky way and the other is our way, of being sure and steady. Of course our way is the better. You will see that we do just as much and make less fuss."

Silvertip came to the edge of the porch and looked around. He was licking his lips, and every bird on the lawn was happy to see that, for it meant that he had just finished his breakfast. His eyes gleamed and his tail waved stiffly as he saw the fat Robins so near. He even crouched down and took four short steps, quivering his body and trying his muscles. Then he remembered how wet the grass was and turned back with a long sigh. After all, his stomach was full and he could afford to wait until the grass was dry. The Robins would be there then, and if they kept on eating Worms at this rate, they would be growing plump and juicy all the time. He began to lick himself all over, as every truly tidy Cat does after eating. By the time he had finished the tip of his tail he was sleepy, so he went into the kitchen and dozed by the fire.

The front door opened with a bang, and the Little Boy stood there, shouting and waving a piece of red paper with a string tied to it. "See my kite!" he cried. "Whee-ee-ee!"

Five birds who had been feeding near flew off in wild alarm. "Now why did he do that?" asked one, after they had settled down elsewhere. Nobody answered. None but Little Boys understand these things, and even they do not always tell.

The Lady came to the door behind him and helped him start away. He proudly carried a small new umbrella, and the precious kite fluttered out behind him. When he was outside the gate, he peeped through it and called back: "Good-by, Mother! I'm going to school to learn everyfing. I'll be a good Boy. Good-by!" Then he ran down the walk with the umbrella held back over his shoulder and the rain falling squarely in his face. All that the birds could see of the Little Boy then was his fat legs bobbing along below the umbrella.

"There!" said all the birds together. "There! Silvertip is asleep and the Little Boy has gone to school. Now we can take comfort."

*   *   *   *   *

When the morning was nearly past, and the birds felt so safe that they had grown almost careless, Silvertip wakened and felt hungry. He walked slowly out of the kitchen door and looked at the grass. The sun was now shining, and it was no longer sparkling with tiny drops. He crept down the steps and around to a place under a big spruce tree, the lower branches of which lay along the ground. A fat Robin was hunting near by.

Silvertip watched her hungrily, and if you were a Cat you might have done exactly the same thing. So you must not blame Silvertip. He was creeping, creeping, creeping nearer, and never looking away from her, when the Little Boy came tramping across the grass. He had come in by the gate of the driveway, and was walking straight toward Silvertip, who neither saw nor heard him.

Then the Little Boy saw what was happening, and

dropped his bright paper chain on the grass beside him. "G'way!" he cried, waving his umbrella. "G'way! Don't you try to eat any birds 'round here. My father doesn't 'low it. G'way! G'way! Else I'll tell my mother that you are a *bad* Cat."

Silvertip fled under the porch, the Robin flew up onto the snowball bush, and all around the birds sang the praises of the good Little Boy with the umbrella. But the Little Boy didn't know this. He stood by the porch and dangled his pretty paper chain until Silvertip forgave him and came out to play. Then they ran together into the house, and the birds heard him shouting, "Mother! Mother! Where are you? I want to give Silvertip some cream. He is so very hungry that he most had to eat up a Robin, only I wouldn't let him."

THE PERSISTENT PHŒBE

IT is not often that a Phœbe will nest anywhere except near running water, and nobody but the Phœbes themselves will ever know why this pair chose to build under a porch of the big house. When they came there on their wedding trip the other birds supposed that they were only visiting, and it was not until a Catbird heard them discussing different porches that any one really believed they might come there to live.

Mrs. Phœbe was eager to begin at once, and could not pass a soft bit of moss or an unusually good blade of grass without stopping to look it over and think how she could weave it in. "I see no use in waiting," said she. "I know just as much about building now as I shall after a while, and I should like a home of my own. It makes my bill fairly tingle to see all these fine grasses and mosses waiting to be used. And the worst of it is," she added, "that if we wait, some other bird may get them instead."

Mr. Phœbe wanted to think it over a little longer. He was older than his wife and had been married before. "Phœbe!" he would exclaim. "Wait a day. You know we are building by a house to please you, now wait one more day to please me."

That, you see, was quite right and perfectly fair, for it is *not* fair for one person to decide everything in a family, and it was right for the wife to wait as long as she could. She could not, of course, wait many days, for there were eggs to be laid, and when it was time for them, the nest had to be ready. Mr. Phœbe knew this and wasted no time.

"We cannot build on a rock," said he, "because there are no rocks here, and we cannot build under a bridge because there is no bridge here. My other wife and I lived under a bridge." Then he stood silent for a long time and looked down at his black feet. When he spoke of his first wife he always seemed sad. The second Mrs. Phœbe had not liked this at first, but he was so good and kind to her, and let her have her own way so much more than some husbands would, that she had begun to feel happier about it.

There is reason to think that she chose an unusual nesting-place just to see how far she could coax him out of his old ways. Perhaps, too, she thought that there would be less in such a place to remind him of his first wife. Another thing which had made her come to feel differently was remembering that if he died or left her she would marry again. Then, you know, she might want to think and talk about her first husband.

She was very proud of him, and watched him as he stood thinking. His upper feathers were deep brown, his under ones a dingy white, and the outer edges of some of his tail-feathers were light colored. His most beautiful features were his black bill and feet and the crest which he could raise on the top of his head. Mrs. Phœbe had the same coloring as her husband, yet she always insisted that he was the better looking of the two, while he insisted, as a good and wise husband should, that she was by far the handsomer.

Now Mr. Phœbe was speaking. "We have decided to build on this house," said he, "and under a porch. Still, there are four large ones and we must find out which is the best. You feed on the shady side and I will feed on the sunny side of the house. Then we shall see how much these people use their porches."

"I'll do it," answered his wife, "but isn't it a pity that there are people living in this house? It would be so much pleasanter if it were empty."

Mrs. Phœbe perched on a maple branch on the shady side and watched two porches. She thought she would like the front one the better, and had already chosen her window ledge, when she noticed a pair of English Sparrows dragging straws and feathers toward it and disappearing inside the cornice. "Not there," she said firmly, as she clutched the branch even more tightly with her pretty black feet. "I will not have quarrelsome neighbors, and I could never bring our children up to be good if the young Sparrows were always near, showing them how to be naughty." Then she darted after a Fly, caught and swallowed him, and was back on her perch.

"I wonder how the back one would do?" she said. "There are no steps leading to it, and those sweetbrier bushes all around it would keep Boys from climbing onto the railing."

She flew near and saw the Maid kneading bread by one window. A door stood open into the big kitchen, and through two other windows she could look into a pleasant dining-room. "I wouldn't mind that," she said. "If I have plenty to eat myself, I would just as soon see other people eating. We like different things anyway. I dare say those people never tasted an insect in their lives and do not even know the flavor of a choice Fly." Then she swallowed a careless Bug who had mistaken her for an English Sparrow and flown when he should have stayed hidden. Mrs. Phœbe was much interested in the nest, but not so much as to let an insect escape. Oh, never so much as that!

Mr. Phœbe watched the back porch on his side. Some Robins were building on a window-ledge there, which he thought exceeding imprudent. But then he was not surprised, for everybody knows how careless Robins are. That is why so many of them have to leave their nests—because they are built where no nest should be. Mr. Phœbe could tell at a glance that no bird should build there. Woodbine climbed over the pillars and fell in a thick curtain from the cornice, and beside the door stood a saucerful of milk. "That means a Cat," said he, "a Cat who stays on this porch most of the time and always comes here when he is hungry. And when he tires of milk he will climb up that woodbine and finish with young Robin. Or, perhaps," he added, "I should say that he will finish *a* young Robin."

The front porch on his side was sunshiny and quiet, but there was the woodbine again, and with the Cat so near. He next looked at the portico over the front door. Under the roof of this was a queer shiny, thin thing with a loop of black thread hanging down in it. He tried to get the thread, but only hit and hurt his bill against the shiny, thin stuff. Then he remembered seeing a bright light in it the night before when he had been awakened by a bad dream. "That will never do," he said. "It is not good for children to sleep with a light near. One would want to be catching insects there, too," he added, "when he should be sleeping. There must be many drawn by the light."

So it ended in the couple building under the dining-room porch on the shelf-like top of a column. Mrs. Phœbe chose this instead of a window-ledge because from here she could look into the window while brooding her eggs. "You may laugh at me all you choose," said she to her husband, "for I did wish the house empty. Since it cannot be, however, I might as well see what the people in it do."

"I was not laughing, my dear," answered her husband meekly (you remember that he had been married before). "I was only smiling with pleasure at our fine nest. You have so much taste in arranging grasses!"

That was the way in which the Phœbes began house-keeping. It was not always easy, sitting on the nest day after day as Mrs. Phœbe had to, with only a chance now and then to stretch her tired legs. She was even glad that people lived in the house. "It gives me something to think about," said she, "although I do get much out of patience with them sometimes. Much they know about bringing up children! That Boy of theirs eats only three times a day. How can they ever hope to raise him unless he eats more? Now, I expect to feed my children all the time, and that is the way to do." Here she darted away to catch a Fly who came blundering along.

"It's a good thing for that Fly that I got him," she said, smilingly. "It saved him from being caught in the Spider's web over there, and I am sure it is much pleasanter to be swallowed whole by a polite Phœbe than to be nibbled at by a horrid Spider."

Mr. Phœbe sometimes brought her a dainty morsel, but he spent much of his time by the hydrant. "There is not much chance to bathe," he said, as he wallowed around in the little pool beside it, "but it is something to smell water. You know we Phœbes like to fly in and out of ponds and rivers, even when we cannot stop for a real bath." His favorite perch was on the top of a tall pole covered with cinnamon vine, in the flower garden. Here he would sit for a whole morning at a time, darting off now and then for an insect, but always returning to the same place and position. He did not even face the other way for a change.

The little Phœbes were hatched much like other birds, and were about as good and about as naughty as children usually are. Mrs. Phœbe was positive that they were remarkable in every way. Mr. Phœbe, having raised other broods, did not think them quite so wonderful, although he admitted that there was not another nestling on the place to compare with them. "Still," as he would modestly remark, "we must remember that we are the only Phœbes here, and that it is not fair to compare them with the young of other birds. You could not expect our neighbors' children to be as bright as they."

Unfortunately there were only two little Phœbes, so each parent could give all his time to one. The mother cared for the son and the father for the daughter. When it was time for them to learn to catch their own Flies, these children did not want to do so. The father made his daughter learn, in spite of the fuss she made. He gave her his old perch on the cinnamon-vine pole, and told her that she must try to catch every insect that flew past. This was after she had been out of the nest several days, and had learned to use her feet and wings.

"If you do not," he said, "I shall not feed you anything." When she pouted her bill, he paid no attention to it, and she soon stopped. There is no use in pouting, you know, unless somebody is looking at you and wishing that you wouldn't. Perhaps it was because he had brought up children before that Mr. Phœbe was so wise.

Mrs. Phœbe meant to be very firm also, but when her son whimpered and said that he couldn't, he knew he couldn't, catch a single one, and that he was sure he would tumble to the ground if he tried it, she always felt sorry for him and said: "Perhaps you can to-morrow." Then she would catch food for him again.

This is how it happened that, day after day, a plump and strong young Phœbe sat on a branch of the syringa bush and let his tired mother feed him. At last his father quite lost patience and interfered. "My dear," he said to his wife, "I will be with our son to-day, and you may have a rest."

"You are very kind," she replied, "but he is so used to having me that I think I might better—"

"I said," interrupted her husband, "that I would be with our son to-day. I advise you to fly away with our daughter and show her something of the world." Mrs. Phœbe did not often hear him speak in that tone of voice. When he did, she always agreed with him.

As soon as father and son were alone, the father said: "Now you are going to catch Flies before sunset. You have let your poor mother nearly work her feathers off for you. (Of course, feathers do not come off so, but this was his way of speaking.) She is very tired, and you are not to act like this again. There comes a Fly. Catch him!"

The young Phœbe made a wild dash, missed his Fly, and came back to the syringa bush whimpering. "I knew I couldn't," he said. "I tried as hard as I could, but he flew away."

"Yes," said his father. "You tried once, just once. You may have to try a hundred times before you catch one, but that is no reason why you should not try. Go for that Mosquito."

The son went, and missed him, of course. This time he knew better than to talk about it. He just flew back to his perch and looked miserable.

"I think you got a little nearer to this one," said his father. "Go for that Fly!"

The young Phœbe was kept darting here and there so often that he had no time to be sulky. Indeed, if people have to keep moving quite fast, they soon forget to want to be sulky. At last he was surprised by his father's tucking a very delicious Bluebottle down his throat. "Just for a lunch," he explained. "Now try for that one."

The son made a sudden lurch and flight, and actually caught him. It was a much smaller Fly than the one which his father had fed him, but it tasted better. He swallowed it as slowly as he could, so as to feel it going down as long as possible. Then he began to be happier. "Watch me catch that Mosquito," he said. And when he missed him, as he did, he made no fuss at all—only said: "I'll get the next one!" When he missed that he simply said: "Well, I'll get the next one, anyhow!"

And he did.

All day long he darted and failed or darted and succeeded, and more and more often he caught the insect instead of missing him.

When the long shadows on the lawn showed that sunset was near, his mother and sister came back. His mother had a delicious morsel for him to eat. "Open your bill very wide," she said, "you poor, tired, hungry child."

He did open his bill, because a Phœbe can always eat a little more anyway, but he did not open it until he had said: "Why, I'm not much tired, and I am not really hungry at all. You just ought to see me catch Flies!"

You can imagine how surprised his mother was. And in the tall fir tree near by he heard a Blackbird say something in a hoarse voice about a persistent Phœbe. But that didn't make much difference, because, you see, he didn't know what "persistent" meant, and if he had known he could not have told whether the Blackbird was talking about him or about his father. Could you have told, if you had been a Phœbe?

THE SAD STORY OF THE
HOG CATERPILLAR

THE grape-vines on the trellis were carefully pruned and tended, but that did not prevent a few Hog Caterpillars of the Vine from making their home upon them. There were a number of other Hog Caterpillars on the place, and all expected to be Hawk Moths when they grew up. Sometimes they thought and talked too much about this, and planned too far ahead. They might better have thought more about being the best kind of Caterpillars. For sometimes, when they were telling what great things they would do by-and-by, they forgot to do exactly as they should just then.

None of them knew when they got their name. Somebody who noticed their small heads and very smooth, fat, and puffy-looking bodies must have begun it. Perhaps, too, this person thought that the queer little things sticking upward and backward from the end of their bodies looked like the tail of a Hog. Those who lived on grape-vines were called Hog Caterpillars of the Vine. Then, when their friends spoke of them, people knew at once to what family they belonged.

If you were to look closely at a Hog Caterpillar of the Vine, you would think him handsome. He has seven reddish spots along the middle of his back, every one set in a patch of pale yellow. On each side you would see a long green stripe with white edges, and below this you would find seven slanting white ones.

When these Hog Caterpillars of the Vine were hatched, they were very, very tiny, and had to feed and rest and change their skins over and over, just as all Caterpillars must. Of course when they changed their skins, they had nobody to help them, because their parents were Hawk Moths and never bothered with the care of children. They believed that Caterpillars should help themselves. "They will have plenty of time to play when they are grown up," the Hawk Moths said, "and it is much better for children to have to change their own skins. If they do that, they will be more careful of their new ones, when they get them."

There is a great deal in the way a child is brought up, and no Caterpillar ever says, "I can't do this;" or, "Somebody must help me get off my old skin, so there!" No indeed! Caterpillars help themselves and make no fuss at all.

This is not saying that they have no faults. It just means that this fault was not one of theirs. Perhaps their worst fault was bragging about what they were going to do. It was either that or carelessness, and every now and then some one of them would be dreadfully punished. With so many hungry birds around, Caterpillars should be very careful. One of those on the grape-vines laughed at a Robin for being afraid of Silvertip. Of course he did not expect to be heard by any except his relatives. He was, though, and as soon as Silvertip had walked off, the Robin came back and hunted for him and ate him. He was very, very sorry for his rudeness, and tried to wriggle out of it, when the Robin spoke about it, but he should have remembered sooner. "I laughed before I thought," he said. "I'll never do it again. Never! Never!"

"Say nothing more about it," answered the Robin, who was noted for his polite ways; "I am very sure you won't." Then he swallowed him while he was talking. The Catbird said that the Robin took in all that the Caterpillar was saying, but the other birds didn't quite understand what he meant by that.

The oldest Hog Caterpillar of the Vine was always reckless. He would feed in plain sight in the sunshine if he wanted to, and he was forever telling what a fine Hawk Moth he expected to be. "If a bird comes after me," he would say, "I will just let go of the leaf and fall to the ground in a little round bunch. I can lie so quietly in the grass that he will never see me." He looked so haughty when saying this that none of his relatives dared to say a word, although a pretty young one wept quietly under her grape-leaf. He had been very attentive to her, and she wanted to marry him after they had changed into Moths. Such plans, you know, might be sadly upset by a hungry and sharp-sighted bird.

Yet birds were not the only people to fear. The Ichneumon Wasps and their cousins the Braconids were always flying around and looking for fat and juicy Caterpillars, and many a promising young fellow had been pounced upon by them. They were so much smaller and more quiet than the birds that they were really much more to be feared. His friends and relatives used to tell the oldest Hog Caterpillar to keep hidden from them, but he paid no attention. "Do you suppose," said he, "that a fine fellow like me is going to sneak under leaves for a slender Ichneumon or a little Braconid? Not I!"

So it is not surprising that when a mother Braconid came along one day, looking for a good place to lay eggs, she saw him busily eating in the sunshine. He had just taken the sixth mouthful from an especially fine leaf when she alighted on him. "Don't move!" she said. "Your position is exactly right. Keep perfectly still and I shall soon be through."

The Hog Caterpillar of the Vine understood every word she said, but he moved as fast as he could. Unfortunately, you know, his legs were all on the under side of his body, and were so stubby that he could not reach up to push her away. He did rub up against a leaf and brush her off for a minute, but she was right back and talking to him again.

"You are very foolish to make such a fuss," she said. "You might better keep still and get it over. I have decided on you, and you can't help yourself. Now hold still!"

There was only one other thing left for the poor Hog Caterpillar of the Vine to do. He let go of the grape leaf and fell to the ground. He had hardly struck it, however, when the Braconid was on his back. "No more nonsense," said she sternly. "You really make me quite out of patience, and I shall not wait any longer. I want to get my eggs laid and have some time for play."

Then she ran her ovipositor, which is the tube through which insects lay their eggs, into his fat back and slipped an egg down through it. How it did hurt! The poor Hog Cater-pillar of the Vine squirmed with pain, and all the Braconid said was: "It would be much easier for me if you would

lie quietly. Still, I am used to working under difficulties....
You won't mind it so after a while." Then she drew out her
ovipositor, stuck it into another place, and laid another egg.

Before she left him, the Braconid had laid thirty-five
eggs in his body, and the Hog Caterpillar of the Vine was
so tired with pain and anger that he could hardly move.
Of the two, perhaps the anger tired him the more. He had
time to do a great deal of thinking before he climbed onto
the vine again. "I will be more careful after this," he said,
"but I guess there isn't any need of telling the other fellows
what has happened. None of them were around when that
dreadful Braconid came."

When he was up on the vine again, one of his relatives
said: "You look sick. What is the matter?" And he answered:
"Oh, I am rather tired. Guess this skin is getting too tight."

The next day he felt quite well, but as time went on he
grew worse and worse. He ate a great deal, yet he did not
grow as he should, and the other Hog Caterpillars of the
Vine began to talk about it. The truth was, you know, that
the Braconid's thirty-five eggs had all hatched, and her
children were eating up the poor Hog Caterpillar of the
Vine. They were fat little Worms then, and when they were
old enough to spin cocoons, they cut thirty-five tiny doors
in his skin and spun their cocoons on the outside.

Then all his relatives and friends knew what was the
matter with him, for wherever he went he had to carry on
his back and sides thirty-five beautiful little shining white
cocoons. He did not think them beautiful, yet they were,
and the Braconid mother looked at them with great pride
as she flew past.

"I should like to see them cut off the tiny round lids of their cocoons," she said, "and fly away, but I suppose I shall not be around then. It is very hard not to have the pleasure of bringing up one's own children. Yet I suppose it is better for them, and one must not be selfish." She flew away with a very good, almost too good, look on her face.

The Hog Caterpillar of the Vine was so tired that he died—what there was left of him. Really the Braconid babies had eaten most of him before spinning their cocoons. The only truly happy people around were the Braconid children, who came out strong and active the next day.

This is all a very, very sad story. It is true, though, and it had to be written, because there may still be some Hog Caterpillars of the Vine, or perhaps some other people, who will not take advice about what they should do, and so they come to trouble.

THE CAT AND THE CATBIRD

IT was late in the fall when Silvertip came to live in the big house, and he was then a very small kitten. All through the winter which followed, he was the pet of the Gentleman and the Lady, of the Maid, and of the people who came there to visit. He liked the Gentleman best and showed it very plainly, but that was only right, for it was the Gentleman, you know, who first brought him into the house.

At night he slept on a red cushion in a basket in the kitchen, except when he made believe catch Mice with a spool for a Mouse. Sometimes, when the other people were in bed, they could hear him running and jumping out there and having the finest kind of a time all by himself. During the days he spent most of his time on a red lamb's-wool rug under a desk where the Lady kept her typewriter. He thought the desk must be a Cathouse, for the room under it was just large enough and just high enough to suit him, and there were walls on three sides to make it warmer. He did not see why the Lady should sit down at it nearly every day and thump-thump-thump on the queer-looking little machine which she kept upstairs in this house. When she did this he had to move farther back on his rug, and it bothered him to do so when he was sleepy.

Sometimes, when he had been really awakened by the thump-thump-thumping of the machine and the ringing of the little bell on it, he would jump up behind it. Then he would peep over its top at the Lady and chew the paper which stuck out in his face until he was gently lifted or pushed away. Sometimes he sat by the side of it, and then he would watch the little bell ringing until he learned to put up one tiny white paw and ring it himself. After he had watched and played in this way for a while, he would lie on the high part of the desk, over where the drawers were, and sleep again. Yet he was never too sleepy to pat with his paws every printed sheet which the Lady took from the machine, or to play with every clean white one which she fastened into it. He liked the white ones the better and didn't see why the Lady wanted to mark them all up so. Still, he thought it was probably her way of playing, so it didn't matter.

Sometimes, when she seemed tired, the Lady would bend over and put her face down against his back and call him "her little collaborator." He did not know what that big word meant. He thought it might be something about his tail. They were both interested in tales.

When the Lady was writing on her lap in the funny way that Ladies sometimes have, he would cuddle down under her portfolio and sleep. For these things he liked her, but she would hardly ever take time to play with him. So, when he heard the latch-key rattle in the front door, he listened, and if it were the Gentleman's step which he heard, he ran to the hall door and waited with his little pink nose to the crack until the Gentleman came in. Then what romps they would have! Back and forth from one room to another, with balls, spools tied onto the most charming strings, and even yardsticks and tape-measures, and things taken from the Lady's sewing-stand.

He liked the Maid, too. She was always kind to him, although she did shut him up one day when he stole a silvery little sardine from the table. She would not let him have anything but milk to eat until he was nearly grown-up. Whenever he smelled a roast or a fine juicy steak he would beg as hard as he knew how, but not one taste did he ever get until he had lost all his Kitten-teeth and his Cat-teeth were growing in. When he was older and knew more about life, he understood that this was to keep him from swallowing a loose tooth with a mouthful of meat, and that Kittens who are given all sorts of food are very likely to do this and bring on fits. You can just imagine what trouble it would make to have a sharp tooth get into a Kitten's stomach.

This was probably the reason, too, why Silvertip grew so very large and handsome. At Christmas time he was given a red ribbon to wear around his neck, red being very becoming to his complexion. He did not care very much for the ribbon, though, and went off into a corner and scratched at it with his hind feet until it came off. Then he chewed it into a wet wisp and left it.

This was Silvertip's life during that first winter. Sometimes on sunshiny days he sat out on the kitchen porch, and once in a while he sunned himself on the broad rail of one of the front porches. Whatever he wanted he had, except, of course, some kinds of food, which he ought not to have anyway. Nobody was ever cross to him and many people were doing things to make him happy. He had yet to learn that this could not last forever.

When spring came he lived more out of doors, and followed the Hired Man around barn and woodshed. He went into the ice-house once, but found that too cold. In these places he saw his first Mice. He will never forget the very first one which he caught. It was just at supper time and he brought it into the kitchen. He could not understand why the Maid should scream and act so queerly. He thought perhaps she wanted it herself.

Whenever the Mouse wriggled or flirted its tail into his eyes he jumped backward. It scared him dreadfully, but he would not let go. Instead of that he would walk backward two or three times around the kitchen range. He wanted to lay the Mouse down and play with it, only he did not know just how to go about it. He tried to have the Maid help him, but every time he went to lay it at her feet she jumped into a chair. At last she called for the Lady. Then the Lady came out and laughed at both of them. How it ended nobody but Silvertip knows, for he walked around the kitchen with it in his mouth until late in the evening, and the next morning there was not a sign of it to be found.

It was this spring, too, that he became acquainted with the Catbird. He heard a queer Cat-like voice saying "Zeay! Zeay!" many times, and yet could never find the Cat to whom it belonged. "Come out here!" he would cry. "Come out here, and we will make believe fight!" When no Cat came he couldn't understand it. He had already become acquainted with many Cats in the neighborhood, and whenever one came to call they made believe fight. It was their favorite game. They would sit around and glare at each other and growl a whole day at a time. So Silvertip could not understand a Cat who said "Zeay!" instead of "Meouw!" and would not fight.

One morning when Silvertip was sitting on the back porch, a slender gray bird, with black crown, tail, bill, and feet, perched on the woodbine over his head and said, "Zeay!" It sounded as though somebody in the little apple-tree had said it, but Silvertip was looking at the bird and saw him open and shut his bill.

"Pht!" said Silvertip, as he began to let his tail and the hair along his back bristle. "Pht! Don't you dare to mock me!"

"Zeay!" answered the bird. "Zeay! Zeay!"

"I don't say it just that way, anyhow," said Silvertip; "so quit!"

"Zeay!" answered the bird.

"I am the Cat who belongs here," said Silvertip. "You quit mocking me or go away!"

"Zeay!" replied the bird, putting his head upon one side. "I am the Catbird who belongs here. I had a nest here last year before you were born, and when I went south for the winter you were not here. Zeay!"

Now Silvertip, not having had a chance to learn much about birds, thought that this one was not telling the truth, and he quite lost his temper. "You deserve to be eaten," he cried, and he began to climb up the woodbine, feeling his way along without taking his eyes from the Catbird. The Catbird sat there and twitched his tail until Silvertip had almost reached him. Then he said, "Zeay!" and flew off. A

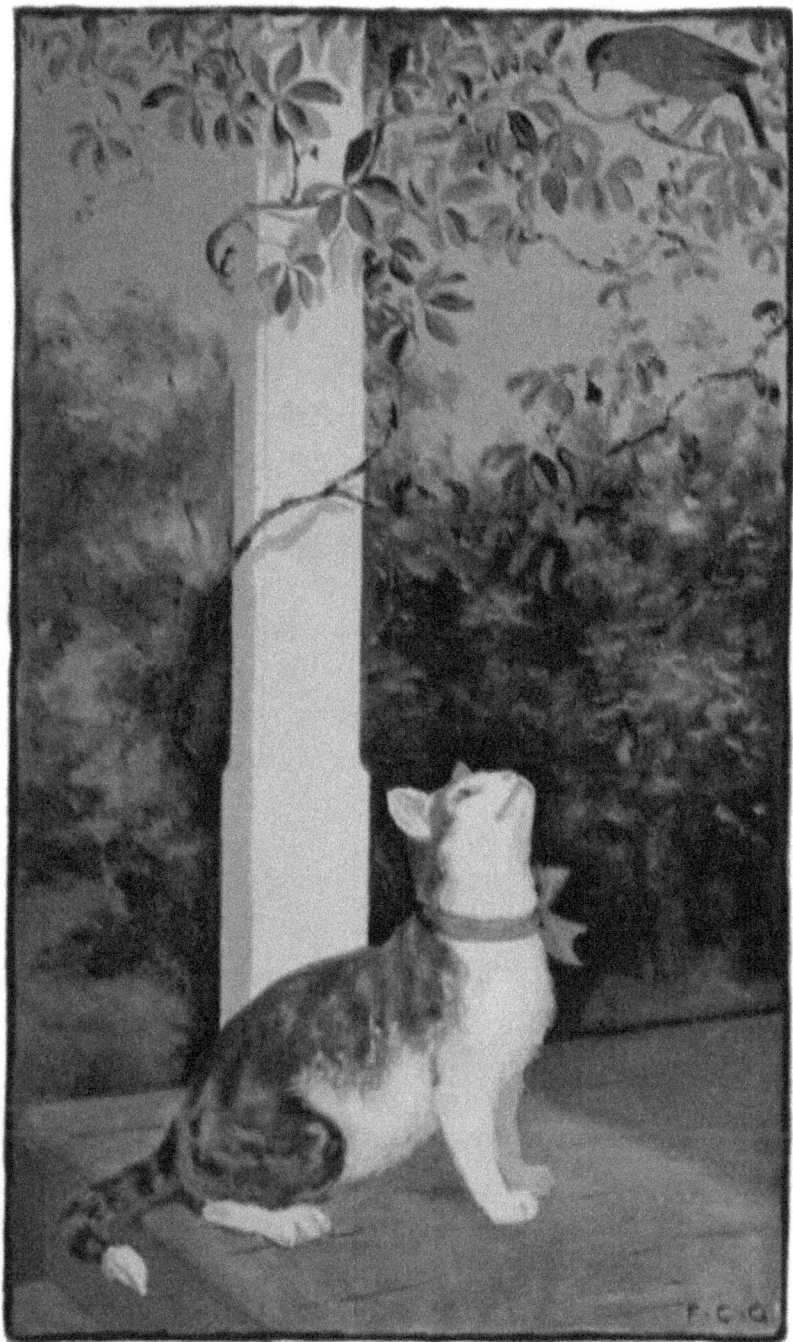

"YOU DESERVE TO BE EATEN."

few minutes later he was sitting on the top twig of a fir tree and singing wonderfully. This was what he sang: "Prut! Prut! Coquillicot! Really! Really! Coquillicot! Hey, Coquillicot! Hey! Victory!"

Silvertip walked back and forth on the kitchen porch. He was too angry to sit down at once. When at last he did, and began to wash himself, he was thinking all the time how mean the Catbird was.

Every day the Catbird came and flirted around and said, "Zeay! Zeay!" till Silvertip lost his temper. He just ached to get his claws into that bird, and that even when his stomach was full. He did not care so much about eating him, you see, although he would undoubtedly have done so if he had had the chance, but he wanted to stop his teasing.

One day he was looking out through a screen door and happened to see the Catbird mocking another bird. He was surprised to hear the other say: "Mock away, if it is any fun! It doesn't hurt me any." Then he heard the Catbird laugh and saw him fly away.

"I wonder what he would do if I were to try that?" said Silvertip. "I believe I will the next time."

That very day, when Silvertip was sunning himself on the porch and heard the same teasing voice say, "Zeay!" above his head, he opened his thick eyelids and slid the other ones about half-way to one side, and looked lazily up. "Pretty good!" he said. "You do a little better every day I think. If you keep at it you can say 'Meouw' after a while." Then he began to shut his eyes again.

"Prut!" exclaimed the Catbird. "It's no fun teasing you any more! You don't care enough about it! Good-by!" And that was the last time that Silvertip ever saw him nearer than the top of a tree. So Silvertip learned one of the great lessons of life, which is not to pay any attention to people who make fun of you, or to mind when you are teased.

THE FRIENDLY BLACKBIRDS

EVER since the year when the first pair of Blackbirds nested near the big house, there had been some of their family in the tall evergreens. One could not truly say that the Blackbirds were popular. When they first came they had a quarrel with a pair of Catbirds about a certain building-place, and most of the older birds took sides with the Catbirds. Nobody knew which couple first chose this place, so of course nobody knows who was really right, and perhaps it might better all be forgotten.

The Blackbirds were happy there and returned the next year with some of their children, who courted and married and built in other tall evergreens in the same yard. After that they were company for each other and had little to do with Robins, Phœbes, and more quiet neighbors. They were handsome, bold, loud-voiced, teasing, and not at all gentle in their ways. Still, that had to be expected of their family. Their neighbors should have remembered that they were not Chipping Sparrows or Humming-birds. On the other hand they were neither Bluejays nor Hawks, and it is much better to think of a bird's good qualities than of his bad ones.

Now, there were so many that nearly every one of the tall

evergreens bore a Blackbird's nest. These were built near the top and close to the trunk of the tree. They were carefully woven of different things and lined with mud. Unless you knew the ways of Blackbirds, you would never find out that there was a nest on the place. No careful Blackbird, you know, will fly straight to his home if any one is watching him. He will walk around on the lawn in the most careless manner possible, until he has the home tree between him and you. Then he will slip noiselessly in under the low branches and make his way to the top by walking around and around the trunk, quite as you would go up a winding staircase.

Two married brothers built in near-by trees and were much together. Their wives were excellent and hard-working birds—almost, but not quite, as good-looking as their husbands. Like them, they were all black except the yellow rings of their eyes. The only difference was that they were smaller and in the sunlight did not have the same gleaming green, blue, and purple lights on their feathers.

These two couples were courting at the same time, and were usually in the same tree, a tall maple. The brothers would sit there in the sunshine, facing the wind and thinking about their sweethearts. Every now and then they would spread their wings and tails, ruffle up their feathers, stand on tiptoe, and squeak in a hoarse voice. Their sweethearts were hiding in trees near by and crept nearer at each squeak.

Mrs. Wren said she had never heard anything like it, and that, much as she loved Mr. Wren, if he had made love to her in that way she would not have married him. "Think," said she, "of singing like a cartwheel in need of oil! And then think of having to listen to that sort of thing right along after you are married!"

"Oh, that part of it will not be so bad," said an experienced Robin. "They probably will not sing so much to their wives."

"Or if they *do* sing," said an Oriole who was building in an apple-tree across the way, "they may go far away from wife and home before beginning. Mr. Oriole will never sing in our own tree. He says he would be seen at once, and then our nest would be found. That is why he always perches near the big house before he begins. You know bright-colored birds have to be very particular."

When the brothers had really won and married their sweethearts, they chose to build as near to each other as possible, and they walked over the lawn together as they hunted for Grubs.

The young wives sat on their eggs and chatted happily with each other. The eggs were bluish-green, with all sorts of queer brown marks. It was very interesting when they were laying them. No two were alike, and then Blackbirds never know how many eggs to expect. It is not with them as it is with other birds, who are sure beforehand of the color and sometimes even of the number.

You can imagine how often the young wives visited each other's nests, and how the one who had only three eggs sat on the other nest, just to see how it would feel to have five under her. Of course this difference meant that the couple who lived in the fir-tree would have to work much harder than the couple in the spruce. Two more mouths take many more Grubs, and Mrs. Spruce-tree Blackbird, as she was sometimes called, could never be sure whether she was glad or sorry that she had only three eggs to hatch. As it happened, it was well for the other family that there were no more.

When the eight little cousins got safely out of their shells and were about as large as Humming-birds, the mother of the fir-tree brood disappeared. She had flown off as usual to find food and nobody ever saw her again. At about this time her neighbors heard a loud bang and saw a red-headed boy pick up something from the road. He put it quickly into his bag and ran away, for he knew that shooting anywhere near the big house was forbidden.

The five motherless nestlings now had only one parent to feed them, and he was a sadly overworked bird. He did the best he could and brought such great billfuls of food that it was a wonder he did not choke himself. He was up early and worked late, yet his five children looked thin and forlorn while their three little cousins were plump and sturdy.

At last Mrs. Spruce-tree Blackbird could stand it no longer. She heard the motherless children crying hungrily when her own three were filled with Grubs almost to the tips of their bills. She paused on the edge of her nest one day with a delicious lunch all ready. Her own children were ready to swallow whatever she should give them, when she suddenly turned and flew over to the fir-tree. "There!" she said, as she tucked food down into first one gaping bill and then another. "There! I guess it won't hurt my own babies, and I know it won't hurt you, if I make them share once in a while."

She spoke with her mouth full, which is bad manners, even in a Blackbird, but one could forgive her still more than that because of the kind things she was saying. When her husband came home she told him what she had done and asked him to help. "Just think of your poor brother," she said. "Our own children will not suffer, and you know how you would feel if you were the one to bring up a family alone." He looked at her lovingly with his yellow eyes, and sidled up close to her on the branch. He was a dreadful tease, as all Blackbirds are, but he was a kind husband and father.

"We will do it," said he. "I really think our own children have eaten too much lately. The eldest one has peeped crossly three times this very day."

"Yes," added Mrs. Blackbird, "I think they have been overfed myself. The baby slept very poorly last night, and kept me awake much of the time by wriggling around under me."

So it was settled, and after that the poor brother had help. His five motherless children began to grow fat and sturdy, while their cousins were none the worse for sharing. Sad to say, however, they made a dreadful fuss because their parents helped feed their little cousins.

"Guess those children could get along some way," they grumbled. "Mother always gives them the best. It isn't fair! We just won't eat if she does that way!"

When she brought them more food they were sulky and told her to take it to the other nest. She looked sharply at them and flew away. "Guess she will feel sorry when we are starved to death," said the three cross nestlings. And when their father came to feed them they acted in the same way.

Their parents, being very wise for a couple with their first brood, did not urge them to eat, or get worried in any way.

They simply paid no attention to them, besides cleaning out the nest once in a while. They also kept on helping the other family. It made them very sad to have their children so foolish and naughty, but they tried to remember how young they were and to be patient.

After a while the three cross children began to feel very badly. Their stomachs had not been really empty since they could remember—not until now. For a while they talked about getting even with their parents. Then they were very still. The baby began to cry. "I am so hungry," said she. And the others cried with her. "So are we," they said.

Their parents flew straight up to the nest. There was nobody watching them, but they were in such haste that they might even have done so if there had been.

"Don't you like to feel hungry?" asked their mother.

"No," sobbed the little Blackbirds. "We want you to feed us."

"What if you had nobody to feed you?" said she. And she never moved toward getting them a Grub.

"B-but we have," they said. "We have a father and a mother."

"Supposing I had been killed," said their mother, "don't you think your aunt would have helped your father care for you?"

"Yes, ma'am," answered all three.

"Then don't you think I ought to help feed your cousins?" said she.

"Yes, ma'am," was the very meek reply.

"Now," said she, "are you willing I should feed your cousins, too?"

"Yes, ma'am," said they, and each was trying to say it first. "We will be good. We won't be cross any more."

Such a meal as the three little Blackbirds had then! It is a wonder that there were not three stomach-aches in that nest at once. When all had been fed and were half asleep under their mother's warm breast, the oldest one said to his sisters: "It must be dreadful not to have enough to eat any of the time. I believe I am glad they fed our cousins."

"We are glad," said the others, and then they went to sleep. So the little Blackbirds learned their first lesson in unselfishness, and they learned it as larger people often have to do, by having a hard time themselves.